Cyber-Torts

R. D. Kelly, B.A., M.S.I.S., D.D., J.D.

cover illustration: Alexandra O. Kelly

Cyber-Torts

is published by:

R. D. Kelly Publishing
c/o R. D. Kelly Law Firm, P.L.L.C.
1420 Fifth Avenue, Suite 2200
Seattle, Washington 98101-1347
robert27522@gmail.com
http://www.rdkellylaw.com/
telephone: (206) 623-3702
Facsimile: (888) 519-4459

ISBN: 978-1-64985-000-3 (paperback)

ISBN: 978-1-64985-001-0 (e-book/Adobe PDF)

ISBN: 978-1-64985-002-7 (EPUB e-book)

Library of Congress Control Number: 2020941709

For licensing information, call, write, or email.

To all the people who have suffered torment

from the internet.

Contents

If men were angels, no government would be necessary.

James Madison

Introduction

The Internet has been in the process of growth since its start in the 1960's. Although the internet has conferred great benefits upon the human race, there have also been problems on the modern internet, including crimes and civil wrongs. Some problems the internet may have amplified have been seen to include online gambling, intellectual property disputes, cyber-defamation, cyber-stalking, cyber-harassment, unauthorized access, pranks, fraud, intentional infliction of emotional distress, intentional interference with business expectancy, and invasion of privacy.

Early in the history of the internet, authorities recognized the need to detect, prosecute, punish, and deter internet crime. There has been much support for controlling crime in cyberspace, but Congress has hampered internet civil law in a misguided effort to give special privileges and immunities to internet companies.

The vast majority of cyber-torts that have been litigated have been litigated in America. American tort law is beginning to evolve to address online injuries such as defamation, invasion of privacy, fraud, spamming and computer trespass.

Some argue that cyber-torts should be considered in the same way as conventional torts. It may be, though, that torts committed with computers on the internet have much greater impact because of the power of the technology. With four billion people having internet access currently and the potentially permanent nature of internet postings, cyber-torts may often be much more serious than conventional torts.

We human beings are vulnerable so the rule of law is required to protect us. The information storage and retrieval capacities of the internet make many benefits possible, but also pose a grave risk of harm. The fallible and imperfect nature of human beings, amplified through the internet, can cause terrible detriment.

A Brief History of Telecommunications Law

Telegraph

The telegraph, which was developed in the United States and Britain during the 1840s, brought tremendous improvement in communication, but also had the potential for misuse (i.e. delay or interception of messages).

Samuel Morse obtained a patent for the telegraph in the United States in 1838.[1] Western Union became a nationwide industrial monopoly, with over 90% of the market share and dominance in every state. State attempts at regulation were largely futile because of the interstate character of the industry. Congress introduced bills in almost every session to either regulate the telegraph industry or allow government entry into it. Western Union's lobby blocked almost any legislation except for those that helped Western Union.

Radio

The sinking on April 15, 1912 of the passenger ship Titanic off the coast of Greenland was a major impetus for passage of the Radio Act of 1912.[2]

The Titanic disaster was made worse because technology had developed faster than regulation. Wireless operators on board the ship had sent an emergency signal and persons in Newfoundland had received the signal. As the news broke, amateur radio operators up and down the U.S. East Coast filled the airwaves with radio noise that prevented the distress signal from being relayed promptly.

There was adequate radio communication, but the proper procedures, including monitoring the frequency and recognizing the priority of emergency traffic, were lacking. The 1912 Act allowed the government to seize control of the broadcast spectrum and assumed responsibility for its allocation among various uses and users.

The Act provided for the licensing of radio operators, a separate frequency for distress calls, absolute priority for distress calls, and twenty-four-hour radio service for ships at sea. The act also required all amateur radio broadcasters to be licensed, and it prohibited them from broadcasting over the main commercial and military wavelengths.

Spectrum scarcity has been used to justify disparate treatment of otherwise protected speech

The Supreme Court has consistently allowed the federal government to impose content-based regulations on broadcast communications, while finding similar regulations constitutionally offensive when applied to print communications.

Because the broadcast spectrum is finite and considered to be public-owned, the Court has used spectrum scarcity to justify this disparate treatment of otherwise protected speech.[3]

The advent of radio opened up the world of broadcasting. To avoid interference between stations, it was necessary for government to license the use of radio frequencies. The landmark Radio Act of 1927 provided basic assumptions forming the foundation for broadcasting policy in the United States to this day. Under the Radio Act, the government (not the licensees) was to hold frequencies used for broadcasting. The government would issue a license only if "the public interest, convenience or necessity" was served. The law established a new Federal Radio Commission which would define what "the public interest" meant. Significantly broadcasters would be held responsible for the content they provided.

The Communications Act of 1934 created the Federal Communications Commission (FCC).[4] In the late 1930s, the FCC investigated the potential for a monopoly on broadcasting.

Telephone

When the telephone was new, it required regulation. Congress first vested federal regulatory authority over telephone services in the Interstate Commerce Commission (ICC), under the Mann-Elkins Act of 1910. The Act extended the authority of the ICC to regulate the telecommunications industry, and designated telephone, telegraph and wireless companies as common carriers. The Mann–Elkins Act paved the way for the Communications Act of 1934 which incorporated the Acts involving telephone service, with those of radio, encompassing all forms of mass communication. This led to the creation of the FCC (Federal Communications Commission) to oversee and regulate the industries.

Television

When television was new, the FCC had to step up and start to regulate it.[5] The Television Branch of the Video Services Division of the FCC licenses and regulates both commercial and noncommercial broadcast UHF and VHF television stations. The Communications Act of 1934, as amended, prescribes the licensing and regulation of television stations in accordance with certain basic requirements. In general, the staff of the Television Branch reviews applications for construction permits, license renewal and assignment of license or transfer of control of the licensee of a television station. The Commission inquires as to whether applicants are legally, technically and financially qualified and whether operation of the proposed station would be in the public interest.

Internet Law History and Fun Facts

Al Gore did not invent the internet.[6] In the 1960's a military program called "ARPANET," was designed to enable computers operated by the military, defense contractors, and universities conducting defense-related research to communicate with one another by redundant channels even if some portions of the network were damaged in a war.[7]

An early case concerning the Internet was *United States v. Morris*.[8] The defendant in Morris was a graduate student who had released an Internet worm that paralyzed thousands of university and military computers throughout the United States.

In *United States v. Riggs*,[9] the Defendant had gained unauthorized access to a Bell South computer and misappropriated proprietary information about the telephone company's 911 system. He subsequently published the confidential data in a hacker newsletter. Riggs pleaded guilty to charges of wire fraud, access code fraud and conspiracy.

In 1994, a plaintiff prevailed in an Internet tort case with a judgment in a controversial landmark decision. An anthropologist had been denied tenure at the University of West Australia in *Rindos v. Hardwick*.[10] A rival anthropologist,

Hardwick, posted a statement online supporting the university's decision and accusing Rindos of sexual deviance and of research detrimental to the aboriginal people of Australia. Dr Rindos was awarded $40,000 in damages from Mr Hardwick.[11]

Although there have been some attempts to draw a distinction between Cyber-Crime and Cyber-Tort, there may be some elements which may be common in both. One main difference is that crime can be punishable by imprisonment, but torts are civil wrongs where the object is obtaining a remedy for a victim (*i.e.* money or a court order). The procedural differences can be significant. For example, a criminal prosecution has the burden of proof beyond a reasonable doubt. A civil plaintiff, on the other hand, only has to prove a case by a preponderance of the evidence. That is a major reason why civil actions have been able to obtain remedies where criminal cases could not (*i.e.* the O. J. Simpson cases).

The Internet has made it easier than ever before to spread a huge amount and variety of information worldwide. As mentioned earlier, websites are often, at a grass root level, a medium for exchanging information between people. Websites can allow any person to write any statement, including a defamatory one, on their own or a third person's virtual profile. The question may then arise about who can be sued by the person against whom such defamatory statement has been made. Traditionally, publishers of false, defamatory statements can be liable.

Many jurisdictions worldwide have wrestled with the relative liability of authors/users versus intermediaries, website holders, and internet service providers as publishers. A major factor to consider is whether such intermediaries knew or should have known about the wrongdoings of users. There may be an analogy between the liability of an internet platform owner and the liability of an owner of premises where unreasonably hazardous conditions existed. Notice can be an important factor. Tort law often allows a jury to determine whether a defendant was liable or not, considering the particular circumstances of a situation. Tort law is usually a matter of common law – a product of court decisions historically. A major factor in cyber-tort law has been the Communications Decency Act of 1996 – 47 U.S.C. §230 (often referred to as "§230" or "Section 230". The effect of §230 has been to immunize internet service providers from civil liability.

It may be that 47 USC §230 will be found unconstitutional because there is a constitutional right to a trial by jury pursuant to the Seventh Amendment. Where §230 deprives a plaintiff of the right to trial by jury, it may be a denial of due process of law.

Important factors to consider should be the degree of control an internet service provider has over content, whether the ISP has notice of wrongdoing, and whether the ISP removed objectionable content from their website upon receiving the notice from the plaintiff.

§230 was passed with practically no opposition. The Communications Decency Act was intended to promote decency on the internet. Instead, courts gutted the Act by declaring the intended censorship to be unconstitutional infringement of freedom of speech. Courts then proceeded to interpret the immunity provisions as giving ISPs carte blanche to allow or prohibit practically anything on the internet. The subsequent abuses have been unsatisfactory and unacceptable.

The interpretation of internet law as being targeted at aiding e-commerce may have been understandable many years ago, but it is time for courts to adjust their interpretation and for Congress to adjust its statutory pronouncements to allow civil law to provide remedies for cyber-torts.

The cases addressing cyber-torts show that American law has not dealt with online offences. The area of legal control of cyber-torts is in its infancy. There is much room for improvement. The area needs serious attention, care, and consideration.

The need for improved cyber-tort law is a worldwide need. Laws of one nation might not be sufficient to fully remedy the situation. Lack of awareness is part of the problem. It can be a vicious circle – lack of remedy leads to unwillingness to complain and lack of complaints leads to lack of remedies. Where cases are going unreported, there can be little awareness of the problem and where there is little awareness of the problem, victims are reluctant to report.

A worldwide problem will have jurisdictional issues, complicating the pursuit of remedies. The universal nature of cyber space, together with its expanding power and reach, may require innovative and fresh approaches to solutions.

Part of the problem may be the less than perfect understanding of technological issues on the part of those who should be responsible for governing. Members of Congress and judges may need further information about the specific details of technological questions. Conversely, technologically savvy people may lack an understanding of judicial and governmental principles and procedures.

Another part of the problem is the dynamic form of interactions on the internet and the constantly progressing and changing status of technology. The capabilities of government to keep things under control needs to struggle to keep up with the rapidly increasing capability of technology to get out of control. The creativity of the human mind, the innovation and industry of human enterprise, are inevitably going to challenge the capacity of the authorities to govern. Nonetheless, government must do its duty to promote justice. This requires diligence, perseverance, and steadfast application.

As of 2020, over 4 billion people are using the Internet (53.6% of the global population).[12] In 2005, only about 1 billion people were internet users.[13] The world is far more interconnected than ever before. Results include working from home and telecommuting. More than half of the global population is now online. The increased affordability and use of cell phones is largely responsible. Of course, the more developed countries have higher rates of internet usage – over 86%.

More Fun Facts

- 300 hours of video are uploaded to YouTube every minute![14]
- Twitter may have approximately 200 billion tweets per year (6,000 tweets per second).[15]

- Youtube, facebook, and twitter are among the most powerful publishers in the world.
- They conduct political censorship.
- Facebook has more than two billion users.
- USA Today has the largest weekday paid circulation in the United States (including digital circulation) at 1,621,091.[16]
- Twitter has 330 million monthly active users.[17]
- Facebook has 1.5 billion daily users.[18]
- Twitter has a market capitalization of over $26 billion.[19]
- Facebook has a market cap of over $644 billion.[20]
- Of the ten most popular websites in the United States as of 2018, six (YouTube, Facebook, Reddit, Wikipedia, Twitter, and eBay) primarily rely on content provided by users.
- Netflix is the only one of the top ten websites that provides mostly its own content.
- Two of the other top ten websites—Google and Yahoo—operate massive search engines that rely on content from third parties.
- Even Amazon, a retailer, has become the trusted consumer brand it is today because it allows users to post unvarnished reviews of products.[21]

- Google has 100 times the market cap of the New York Times and perhaps 100 times the influence.[22]
- The social media companies are bigger than the automobile companies.[23]

Case Law Before Section 230

In *Farmers Educational & Cooperative Union of America, North Dakota Division v. WDAY, Inc.*,[24] a defamation suit did not lie against a radio station that allowed a political candidate to speak where the station had a statutory requirement to allow the candidate to speak.

In *Smith v. California*,[25] a bookseller was not guilty of the crime of possessing an obscene book where the bookseller did not know of the book's contents. The judicial interpretations of the First Amendment established there was sometimes a need to protect not only speakers and publishers but also the passive distributors of information.[26],[27]

Cubby v. CompuServe[28]

Disputes began to arise regarding online communication bulletin boards as early as 1990.[29]

Cubby sued CompuServe for libel, business disparagement, and unfair competition, alleging a third party had posted defamatory statements. The court used standard of liability for CompuServe as whether it knew or had reason to know of the allegedly defamatory statements. Such a factor is sometimes considered in premises liability cases. CompuServe was treated like a public library, bookstore, or newsstand.

CompuServe won because it had merely been a distributor of the content and had not interfered in the process, posted anything, or participated in the creation of content.

Stratton Oakmont v. Prodigy Services Co.[30]

The *Stratton* court held that Prodigy was liable as the publisher of defamatory content created by its users because it exercised editorial control over the messages on their bulletin boards in three ways: 1) by posting Content Guidelines for users, 2) by enforcing those guidelines with "Board Leaders", and 3) by utilizing screening software designed to remove offensive language.

The court's general argument for holding Prodigy liable, in the face of the CompuServe case, was that Prodigy's conscious choice, to gain the benefits of editorial control, had opened it up to a greater liability than CompuServe and other computer networks that make no such choice.

Prodigy had promoted its self-regulation, family friendly policies, content moderation, and editorial control as selling points. Commentators have noted that there may be economic benefits and business advantages for providers of interactive computer services who work to exclude racist or obscene content.

The Enactment of §230

The *Stratton Oakmont* decision and the attention it received were significant in the imminent action of Congress in enacting §230. The Communications Act of 1934, codified as Chapter 5 of Title 47 of the United States Code, 47 U.S.C. § 151 et seq. was amended by the Telecommunications Act of 1996.[31]

During the congressional deliberations, Representative Cox made the following comments:

> "I will give you two quick examples: A Federal court in New York, in a case involving CompuServe, one of our on-line service providers, held that CompuServe would not be liable in

a defamation case because it was not the publisher or editor of the material. It just let everything come onto your computer without, in any way, trying to screen it or control it. "But another New York court, the New York Supreme Court, held that Prodigy, CompuServe's competitor, could be held liable in a $200 million defamation case because someone had posted on one of their bulletin boards, a financial bulletin board, some remarks that apparently were untrue about an investment bank, that the investment bank would go out of business and was run by crooks. "Prodigy said, 'No, no; just like CompuServe, we did not control or edit that information, nor could we, frankly. We have over 60,000 of these messages each day, we have over 2 million subscribers, and so you cannot proceed with this kind of a case against us.' "The court said, 'No, no, no, no, you are different; you are different than CompuServe because you are a family-friendly network. You advertise yourself as such. You employ screening and blocking software that keeps obscenity off of your network. You have people who are hired to exercise an emergency delete function to keep that kind of material away from your subscribers. You don't permit nudity on your system. You have content guidelines. You, therefore, are going to face higher, stric[t]er liability because you tried to exercise some control over offensive material.' "Mr. Chairman, that is backward. We want to encourage people like Prodigy, like CompuServe, like America Online, like the new Microsoft network, to do everything possible for us, the customer, to help us control, at the portals of our computer, at the front door of our house, what comes in and what our children see. This technology is very quickly becoming available, and in fact every one of us will be able to tailor what we see to our own tastes. . . . "Mr. Chairman, our amendment will do two basic things: First, it will protect computer Good Samaritans, online service providers, anyone who provides a front end to the Internet, let us say, who takes steps to screen indecency and offensive material for their customers. It will protect them from taking on liability such as occurred in the Prodigy case in New York that they should not face for helping us and for helping us solve this problem. Second, it will establish as the policy of the United States that we do not wish to have content regulation by the Federal Government of what is on the Internet . . . ." (141 Cong. Rec. H8469- H8470 (daily ed. Aug. 4, 1995).)[32]

§230 passed into law with relatively little opposition. Many members of Congress were focused on the telephone and broadcast implications of the CDA. The internet was too new to notice. The light touch for a new industry seemed acceptable at the time and received support from both civil liberties groups and family-oriented groups.

Congress was intentionally overruling *Stratton Oakmont*. It passed the House in a 414 – 16 vote and the Senate in a 91 – 5 vote. There was little media mention of §230.

Two extremely significant portions of §230 are subsections (c)(1) and (c)(2).

Section 230(c)(1) essentially immunizes internet service providers for under-screening. It says **"[n]o provider or user of an interactive computer service shall be treated as the publisher or speaker of any information provided by another information content provider"**. As we shall see, those words have been interpreted broadly to provide immunity to internet service providers to a great extent.

Section 230(c)(2) essentially immunizes internet service providers for over-screening.

Reno v. American Civil Liberties Union[33]

Other provisions of the CDA failed to pass constitutional muster with the U.S. Supreme Court because certain words in the provisions were unacceptably vague. The 1997 case of *Reno v. American Civil Liberties Union* invalidated certain portions of the CDA on the basis of First Amendment rights. In 1997, the Court found it necessary to explain that "The Internet is an international network of interconnected computers".

The court noted how the volume and range of Internet communications made the "heckler's veto" a real threat under the Court of Appeal's holding. The United States Supreme Court cautioned against reading the CDA to confer unlimited power of censorship on those offended by Internet speech.[34]

Cases Strengthening § 230

Zeran v. America Online[35]

The 1997 case of *Zeran v. America Online, Inc.*[36] was one of the first to interpret the new Section 230. It has been described as the most important case in internet law.[37] There have been some horrible pranks on the internet. Such cases have given rise to lawsuits based on allegations of negligence on the part of the ISP.

The facts, as described by the court, are the following:

On April 25, 1995, an unidentified person posted a message on an AOL bulletin board advertising "Naughty Oklahoma T-Shirts." The posting described the sale of shirts featuring offensive and tasteless slogans related to the April 19, 1995, bombing of the Alfred P. Murrah Federal Building in Oklahoma City. Those interested in purchasing the shirts were instructed to call "Ken" at Zeran's home phone number in Seattle, Washington. As a result of this anonymously perpetrated prank, Zeran received a high volume of calls, comprised primarily of angry and derogatory messages, but also including death threats. Zeran could not change his phone number because he relied on its availability to the public in running his business out of his home. Later that day, Zeran called AOL and informed a company representative of his predicament. The employee assured Zeran that the posting would be removed from AOL's bulletin board but explained that as a matter of policy AOL would not post a retraction. The parties dispute the date that AOL removed this original posting from its bulletin board.

On April 26, the next day, an unknown person posted another message advertising additional shirts with new tasteless slogans related to the Oklahoma

City bombing. Again, interested buyers were told to call Zeran's phone number, to ask for "Ken," and to "please call back if busy" due to high demand. The angry, threatening phone calls intensified. Over the next four days, an unidentified party continued to post messages on AOL's bulletin board, advertising additional items including bumper stickers and key chains with still more offensive slogans. During this time period, Zeran called AOL repeatedly and was told by company representatives that the individual account from which the messages were posted would soon be closed. Zeran also reported his case to Seattle FBI agents. By April 30, Zeran was receiving an abusive phone call approximately every two minutes.

Meanwhile, an announcer for Oklahoma City radio station KRXO received a copy of the first AOL posting. On May 1, the announcer related the message's contents on the air, attributed them to "Ken" at Zeran's phone number, and urged the listening audience to call the number. After this radio broadcast, Zeran was inundated with death threats and other violent calls from Oklahoma City residents. Over the next few days, Zeran talked to both KRXO and AOL representatives. He also spoke to his local police, who subsequently surveilled his home to protect his safety. By May 14, after an Oklahoma City newspaper published a story exposing the shirt advertisements as a hoax and after KRXO made an on-air apology, the number of calls to Zeran's residence finally subsided to fifteen per day.

Zeran first filed suit on January 4, 1996, against radio station KRXO in the United States District Court for the Western District of Oklahoma. On April 23, 1996, he filed this separate suit against AOL in the same court. Zeran did not bring any action against the party who posted the offensive messages.[1] After Zeran's suit against AOL was transferred to the Eastern District of Virginia pursuant to 28 U.S.C. § 1404(a), AOL answered Zeran's complaint and interposed 47 U.S.C. § 230 as an affirmative defense. AOL then moved for judgment on the pleadings pursuant to Fed. R. Civ. P. 12(c). The district court granted AOL's motion, and Zeran filed this appeal.

In affirming the decision, the 4th Circuit was aware that according to traditional common law, publishers can be held liable for defamatory statements contained in their works even absent proof that they had specific knowledge of the statement's inclusion.[38] The court was also aware that Zeron maintained AOL made it impossible to identify the original party by failing to maintain adequate records of its users. Zeran argued that the § 230 immunity eliminated only publisher liability, leaving distributor liability intact. Zeran contended that decisions like *Stratton Oakmont* and Cubby recognized a legal distinction between publishers and distributors which imposed liability on publishers in general and distributors if they had notice of the wrongful content. (Reason would recognize the presence of the distinct notice element in distributor liability.) Zeran contended that interpreting § 230 to impose liability on service providers with knowledge of defamatory content on their services was consistent with the statutory purposes outlined in Part IIA. Zeran contended that the interpretive canon favoring retention of common law principles unless Congress speaks directly to the issue counsels a restrictive reading of the § 230 immunity.

The court was also aware of the New York state court decision, *Stratton Oakmont, Inc. v. Prodigy Servs. Co.*[39] where the plaintiffs sued Prodigy--an interactive computer service like AOL--for defamatory comments made by an unidentified party on one of Prodigy's bulletin boards, that the court held Prodigy to the strict liability standard normally applied to original publishers of defamatory statements, rejecting Prodigy's claims that it should be held only to the lower "knowledge" standard usually reserved for distributors, and that the court reasoned that Prodigy acted more like an original publisher than a distributor both because it advertised its practice of controlling content on its service and because it actively screened and edited messages posted on its bulletin boards.

Zeran v. Diamond Broadcasting[40]

In the parallel case against the radio station's parent company, the court elaborated on the heinous nature of the prank as a "bulletin board announcing the availability for sale of

'Naughty Oklahoma T-Shirts,' bearing such slogans, to repeat only the least offensive, as 'Rack'em, Stack'em and Pack'em—Oklahoma 1995' and 'Visit Oklahoma—it's a Blast.' Another slogan crudely referenced the children who died in the bombing." The opinion further elaborates on the particular circumstances by saying the following:

> Defendant owns KRXO, a classic-rock radio station in Oklahoma City. On April 29, 1995, an AOL member sent an e-mail containing a copy of the original, April 25th posting to one of KRXO's on-air personalities, Mark ("Shannon") Fullerton, who, together with Ron ("Spinozi") Benton, hosted the "Shannon & Spinozi Show," a drive-time morning show, which usually consisted of light-hearted commentary, humor, and games. In the aftermath of the bombing, and continuing for a period of four to six weeks thereafter, however, the show had become a forum for discussion of the bombing and expression of the emotions it aroused. Its tone was serious and somber.

Shannon first saw the e-mail either late in the evening on the day it was sent or early the next morning, May 1, 1995. Shannon was an AOL member and had given his screen name out over the air to enable his listeners to send messages to him. He did not know the person who sent the posting.

Before beginning his shift on May 1, Shannon unsuccessfully attempted to e-mail Ken ZZO3 through AOL, but received a pop-up message informing him that the addressee was not a known AOL member. He did not attempt to call the telephone number on the posting, purportedly because it was before business hours.

Shannon then went on air, discussing the posting, reading the slogans, and reading Plaintiff's telephone number. Shannon urged his listeners to call Ken ZZ03 and tell Ken ZZ03 what they thought of him for offering such products. On that day, Plaintiff received approximately 80 angry, obscenity-laced calls from the Oklahoma City area, including death threats. Plaintiff described it as the worst day of his life and, shortly thereafter, involved law enforcement. The anxiety Plaintiff felt as a result eventually led him to visit his family physician, who treated Plaintiff by prescribing an anti-anxiety drug.

Although most of the callers hung up before Plaintiff had an opportunity to speak, Plaintiff was able to learn that the posting had been mentioned on KRXO. Plaintiff called KRXO and asked that KRXO broadcast a retraction, which it did.

Plaintiff does not know of anyone who knows him by the name Kenneth Zeran who saw the AOL postings, heard the broadcast, or associated him with "Ken Z" or the phone number on the AOL postings.

Although the Zeran decisions may have been appropriate at the time, things have changed considerably since then. Instead of nurturing fledgling startup enterprises, Section 230 currently provides a palace guard for some of our favorite billionaires while the innocent victims of vicious internet misdeeds continue to suffer.

Critics have condemned the *Zeran* decisions for giving insufficient consideration to the interests of defamation victims.[41] Commentators have said that Zeran imposed First Amendment goals on legislation that was actually adopted for the speech-restrictive purpose of controlling the dissemination of content over the Internet.

Blumenthal v. Drudge and AOL

In *Blumenthal v. Drudge and AOL*[42], the court followed *Zeran* in interpreting Section 230 as an ironclad, water-tight, air-tight immunity, notwithstanding the fact that AOL had hired a writer who wrote extraordinarily false, defamatory material.

The decision had the effect of immunizing online intermediaries even though the judge seemed to recognize that the end result was unfair. *Blumenthal* was a year after the *Zeran* decision.

As an indication of how different things were in 1998, the court felt it necessary to explain what a "hyperlink" was.

Blumenthal was an early application of Section 230 of the CDA. The early Internet case involved AOL, Matt Drudge of the Drudge

Report and an assistant to Bill Clinton in the White House, Sidney Blumenthal. Matt Drudge was an early Internet blogger who often produced tabloid and rumor stories about public figures in Washington. AOL had a contractual arrangement with Drudge by which it paid him $3,000 per month - Drudge's sole income at the time to carry his reports, and retained the right to remove, or direct Drudge to remove, any content which, as reasonably determined by AOL violated AOL's then-standard Terms of Service. In other words, AOL reserved to itself the right to act as a publisher in determining whether content offered by Drudge met AOL's editorial standards.

Drudge allegedly posted false statements about Blumenthal being involved in marital disputes and abuse. On August 10, 1997, Drudge had transmitted the report from Los Angeles, California by email to his direct subscribers and posted the information about Blumenthal on AOL, which was hosting the Drudge Report at the time. After receiving a letter from plaintiffs' counsel on August 11, 1997, Drudge retracted the story through a special edition of the Drudge Report posted on AOL and emailed to his subscribers. Drudge later publicly apologized to the Blumenthals, Nonetheless, Blumenthal and his wife filed a defamation lawsuit on August 27, 1997, claiming libel and serious harm to reputation and asking for $30 million from Drudge and his employer America Online (AOL).

In October 1997, Drudge and AOL filed motions for summary judgment. On April 22, 1998, the court refused to dismiss the case against Drudge, finding that the court had personal jurisdiction over him, but granted AOL's motion on the basis that AOL was immune from liability under section 230 of the Communications Decency Act.

During a discovery dispute in April 1999, the federal district court applied the constitutional reporter's privilege to Drudge and denied Blumenthal access to information about Drudge's sources.

Blumenthal eventually reached a settlement with Drudge in early 2001. Apparently, Blumenthal claimed he was forced to settle because he could no longer financially afford the suit.

On May 9, 2001, the parties filed a stipulation of voluntary dismissal.[43]

Doe v. America Online

A Florida Supreme Court 2001 decision, *Doe v. America Online*[44] had an even more alarming situation. The court set forth the facts by saying the following:

Doe filed a complaint in 1997 against Richard Lee Russell and America Online (AOL), an Internet service provider (ISP), to recover for alleged emotional injuries suffered by her son, John Doe. Doe claimed that in 1994 Russell lured John Doe, who was then eleven years old, and two other minor males to engage in sexual activity with each other and with Russell. She asserted that Russell photographed and videotaped these acts and used AOL's "chat rooms" to market the photographs and videotapes and to sell a videotape. Doe did not allege that Russell transmitted photographs or images of her son via the AOL service. In her six-count complaint, Doe claimed that AOL violated criminal statutes, section 847.011 and section 847.0135(2), Florida Statutes (1993). She alleged that AOL was negligent per se in violating section 847.0135, Florida Statutes, by allowing Russell to distribute an advertisement offering "a visual depiction of sexual conduct involving [John Doe]" and by allowing Russell to sell or arrange to sell child pornography, thus aiding in the sale and distribution of child pornography, including obscene images of John Doe. Doe asserted a separate claim for negligence based on the allegation that AOL knew or should have known that Russell and others like him used the service to market and distribute child pornography; that it should have used reasonable care in its operation; that it breached its duty; and that the damages to John Doe were reasonably foreseeable as a result of AOL's breach. Doe further claimed that complaints had been communicated to AOL as to Russell's transmitting obscene and unlawful photographs or images and that although AOL reserved the right to terminate without notice the service of any member who did not abide by its "Terms of Service and Rules of the Road," AOL neither warned Russell to stop nor suspended his service. Two of the counts in Doe's complaint were directed at Russell.

AOL moved to dismiss Doe's complaint and argued, inter alia, that Doe's claims were barred by 47 U.S.C. § 230 (Supp. II 1996), in that section 230 prohibits civil actions that treat an interactive computer service as the "publisher or speaker" of messages transmitted over its service by third parties. The trial court granted AOL's motion to dismiss with prejudice, finding that the immunity Congress provided for interactive computer services in section 230 applied to Doe's claims. The Fourth District Court of Appeal affirmed and held that the trial court's conclusion was consistent with *Zeran v. America Online, Inc.*, 129 F.3d 327 (4th Cir.1997), in which the federal circuit court held that "Congress' desire [in enacting 47 U.S.C. § 230] to promote unfettered speech must supersede conflicting common law causes of action." Id. at 334. The Fourth District certified the questions of great public importance to this Court.

The majority followed *Zeran* and affirmed, but *Doe v AOL* was a 4-3 decision and the dissent was vigorous indeed. Judge Lewis wrote that "because the analysis upon which it [*Zeran*] is based is faulty and leads to a totally unacceptable interpretation, it should not be followed". Further, the dissent opined that the majority had transformed the so-called "Decency Act" "from an appropriate shield into a sword of harm and extreme danger which places technology buzz words and economic considerations above the safety and general welfare of our people."

As a final note, the dissent wrote the following:

> The absurd implications of *Zeran* are contrary to the very core of the Communications Decency Act, which, through section 509 of the Telecommunications Act of 1996 (entitled "On-line Family Empowerment") added § 230 (entitled "Protection for private blocking and screening of offensive material"). As stated in one legal commentary:
> The result [in *Zeran*] gives an ironic twist to Congress' response to *Stratton Oakmont*:

Cyber-Torts
Page 45

information service providers can not incur liability for their failure to monitor content, because to hold otherwise would provide them with an incentive to fail to monitor content! The CDA's protective umbrella, intended for "good Samaritan" monitors, turns out also to shield those who can not or will not provide such a service.[45]

Schneider v. Amazon.com, Inc.

In *Schneider v. Amazon.com, Inc.*,[46] the court dismissed plaintiff's claims on the supposition that § 230 granted immunity to Amazon.com for comments about a book plaintiff had published through Amazon.

Batzel v. Smith[47]

The *Batzel* case showed Courts also will grant immunity even if the online intermediary modified the third-party content (provided the modification was not the source of the harmful content). Smith was a handyman who had a disagreement about some cabinet work he had done for Batzel. Smith sent an email to a museum security listserv wherein he alleged Batzel was the granddaughter of one of Adolph

Hitler's "right-hand men", Heinrich Himmler. Smith further alleged he saw artwork in Batzel's home that he believed had been looted from Jewish people during World War II. After making minor edits to the email, the group sent it to its members on the listserv, and posted the edited message on its website. Batzel sued the museum security group for defamation. The Ninth Circuit ruled that Section 230 applied. The Court reasoned the museum group's "minor alterations" to the email did not necessarily render it responsible for the content created by the handyman (Smith), provided the group's employee reasonably concluded that the email was intended for publication. The Court wrote Section 230 "necessarily precludes liability for exercising the usual prerogative of publishers to choose among proffered material and to edit the material published while retaining its basic form and message."

The opening sentence of Judge Berzon's opinion says "There is no reason inherent in the technological features of cyberspace why First Amendment and defamation law should apply differently in cyberspace than in the brick and mortar world" and then goes on the follow *Zeran*. The Court did, however admit that "the broad immunity created by § 230 can sometimes lead to troubling results" (*citing Blumenthal*).

The Court saliently noted the following:

One possible solution to this statutorily created problem is the approach taken by Congress in the Digital Millennium Copyright Act ("Digital Act"). The Digital Act includes immunity provisions, similar to those of the Communications Decency Act, that protect service providers from liability for content provided by third parties. The Digital Act, however, unlike the Communications Decency Act, provides specific notice, takedown, and put-back procedures that carefully balance the First Amendment rights of users with the rights of a potentially injured copyright holder. See 17 U.S.C. §§ 512(c) and (g); see also H.R. Rep. No. 105-551, at 52-62 (1998) (describing the DMCA's take-down and put-back procedures); Comm. Print, Section-By-Section Analysis of H.R. 2281, at 25-36 (Sept. 1998) (same). To date, Congress has not amended § 230 to provide for similar take-down and put-back procedures.

Judge Gould wrote a partial dissent. He believed that Judge Berzon's reading of Section 230 was far too generous to defendants and that the statute should apply only if the defendant "took no active role" in choosing third-party content. Judge Gould opined that Congress had not wanted the new frontier of the internet to be like the Old West: a lawless zone governed by retribution and mob justice, the CDA should not license anarchy, a "person's decision to disseminate the rankest rumor or most blatant falsehood should not escape legal redress merely because the person chose to disseminate it through the Internet rather than through some other medium."

Part of the significance of the *Batzel* case is the location in the 9th Circuit – the home of Silicon Valley, Amazon, and Microsoft.[48]

It is also significant that the court in *Batzel* suggested that Congress might provide notice, "takedown," and "put-back" procedures similar to those in the DMCA as a way of limiting the broad scope of section 230 immunity, which currently gives service providers little incentive to remove defamatory postings.[49] Congress has not responded.

Carafano v. Metrosplash[50,51]

"[D]espite the serious and utterly deplorable consequences that occurred in this case", the 9th Circuit concluded that Congress intended that service providers such as the Defendant be afforded immunity from suit.

The Court's opinion commences as follows:

> This is a case involving a cruel and sadistic identity theft. In this appeal, we consider to what extent a computer match making service may be legally responsible for false content in a dating profile provided by someone posing as another person. Under the circumstances presented by this case, we conclude that the service is statutorily immune pursuant to 47 U.S.C. § 230(c) (1).
>
> *   Matchmaker.com is a commercial Internet dating service. For a fee, members of Matchmaker post anonymous profiles and may then view profiles of other members in their area, contacting them via electronic mail sent through the Matchmaker server. A typical profile contains one or more pictures of the subject, descriptive information such as age, appearance and interests, and answers to a variety

of questions designed to evoke the subject's personality and reason for joining the service.

Members are required to complete a detailed questionnaire containing both multiple-choice and essay questions. In the initial portion of the questionnaire, members select answers to more than fifty questions from menus providing between four and nineteen options. Some of the potential multiple choice answers are innocuous; some are sexually suggestive. In the subsequent essay section, participants answer up to eighteen additional questions, including "anything that the questionnaire didn't cover." Matchmaker policies prohibit members from posting last names, addresses, phone numbers or e-mail addresses within a profile. Matchmaker reviews photos for impropriety before posting them but does not review the profiles themselves, relying instead upon participants to adhere to the service guidelines.

On October 23, 1999, an unknown person using a computer

in Berlin posted a "trial" personal profile of Christianne Carafano in the Los Angeles section of Matchmaker. (New members were permitted to post "trial" profiles for a few weeks without paying.) The posting was without the knowledge, consent or permission of Carafano. The profile was listed under the identifier "Chase529."

Carafano is a popular actress. Under the stage name of Chase Masterson, Carafano has appeared in numerous films and television shows, such as "Star Trek: Deep Space Nine," and "General Hospital." Pictures of the actress are widely available on the Internet, and the false Matchmaker profile "Chase529" contained several of these pictures. Along with fairly innocuous responses to questions about interests and appearance, the person posting the profile selected "Playboy/Playgirl" for "main source of current events" and "looking for a one-night stand" for "why did you call." In addition, the open-ended essay responses indicated that "Chase529" was looking for a "hard and dominant" man with "a strong sexual appetite" and that she "liked sort of be []ing controlled by a man, in and out of bed." The profile text did not include a last name for "Chase" or indicate Carafano's real name, but it listed two of her movies (and, as mentioned, included pictures of the actress).

In response to a question about the "part of the LA area" in which she lived, the profile provided Carafano's home address. The profile included a contact e-mail address, cmla2000@yahoo.com, which, when contacted, produced an automatic e-mail reply stating, "You think you are the right one? Proof it!!" [sic], and providing Carafano's home address and telephone number.

Unaware of the improper posting, Carafano soon began to receive messages responding to the profile. Although she was traveling at the time, she checked her voicemail on October 31 and heard two sexually explicit messages. When she returned to her home on November 4, she found a highly threatening and sexually explicit fax that also threatened her son. Alarmed, she contacted the police the following day. As a result of the profile, she also received numerous phone calls, voicemail messages, written correspondence, and e-mail from fans through her professional e-mail account. Several men expressed concern that she had given out her address and phone number (but simultaneously expressed an interest in meeting her). Carafano felt unsafe in her home, and she and her son stayed in hotels or away from Los Angeles for several months.

Sometime around Saturday, November 6, Siouxzan Perry, who handled Carafano's professional website and much of her e-mail correspondence, first learned of the false profile through a message from "Jeff." Perry exchanged e-mails with Jeff, visited the Matchmaker site, and relayed information about the profile to Carafano. Acting on Carafano's instructions, Perry contacted Matchmaker and demanded that the profile be removed immediately. The Matchmaker employee indicated that she could not remove the profile immediately because Perry herself had not posted it, but the company blocked the profile from public view on Monday morning, November 8. At 4:00 AM the following morning, Matchmaker deleted the profile.

Carafano filed a complaint in California state court against Matchmaker and its corporate successors, alleging invasion of privacy, misappropriation of the right of publicity, defamation, and negligence. The defendants removed the case to federal district court. The district court granted the defendants' motion for summary judgment in a published opinion. *Carafano v. Metrosplash.com, Inc.*, 207 F. Supp. 2d 1055 (C.D. Cal. 2002). The court rejected Matchmaker's argument for immunity under 47 U.S.C. § 230(c) (1) after finding that the company provided part of the profile content. *Id.* at 1067-68.

However, the court rejected Carafano's invasion of privacy claim on the grounds that her home address was "newsworthy" and that, in any case, Matchmaker had not disclosed her address with reckless disregard for her privacy. *Id.* at 1069. Similarly, the court rejected Carafano's claims for defamation, negligence, and misappropriation because she failed to show that Matchmaker had acted with actual malice. *Id.* at 1073-76.

Carafano timely appealed. America Online, eBay, and two coalitions of online businesses intervened to challenge the district court's construction of § 230(c) (1). Several privacy advocacy groups and two organizations representing entertainers intervened in support of Carafano.

The Court followed the *Batzel* and *Zeran* cases, *inter alia* and held that a Web-based dating-service provider was not liable when an unidentified party posted a false online personal profile for a popular actress, causing her to receive sexually explicit phone calls, letters, and faxes at her home. Acknowledging that the immunity provision in § 230(c)(1) of the CDA causes Internet publishers to be treated differently from corresponding publishers in print, television and radio, the Court said "so long as a third party willingly provides the essential published content, the interactive service provider receives full immunity regardless of the specific editing or selection process."

The Wikipedia Seigenthaler Incident

An unregistered Wikipedia user, on May 26, 2005, created a five-sentence biographical article about John Seigenthaler (journalist, writer, political figure, and a founding editorial director of USA Today) that contained false and defamatory content.[52] The false statement in Seigenthaler's Wikipedia article read:

> John Seigenthaler Sr. was the assistant to Attorney General Robert Kennedy in the early 1960s. For a brief time, he was thought to have been directly involved in the Kennedy assassinations of both John, and his brother, Bobby. Nothing was ever proven.

When he was alerted of the article's existence, Seigenthaler directly contacted Wikipedia co-founder Jimmy Wales, who removed the false claims. As Seigenthaler later wrote: "For four months, Wikipedia depicted me as a suspected assassin before Wales erased it from his website's history".

Seigenthaler later wrote an op-ed on the experience for USA Today in which he wrote, "And so we live in a universe of new media with phenomenal opportunities for worldwide communications and research – but populated by volunteer vandals with poison-pen intellects. Congress has enabled them and protects them"

Barrett v. Rosenthal[53]

Rosenthal posted a copy of an allegedly defamatory article on the Web sites of two newsgroups which had no administrators and no one to enforce rules of conduct. The trial court ruled that the republication was immunized by section 230(c)(1). The Court of Appeals reversed, saying Rosenthal was not immune from liability as a "distributor" under the common law of defamation. The California Supreme Court reversed on §230 grounds, but the court admitted that "recognizing broad immunity for defamatory republications on the Internet has some troubling consequences."

Reacting to the Court of Appeals decision, one proposed elaborate reconstruction of §230, proceeding from the premise that Congress did not intend to immunize users of the internet who maliciously republish libelous content, was set forth by James Jenal.[54] Jenal posited four categories of "users," Readers, Posters, Moderators, and Administrators, and recommended depriving Posters of immunity.[55] According to the court in *Barrett v. Rosenthal,* no court had at that time attempted such an adventurous reading of §230 noting the provision had received a narrow, textual construction, not one that has welcomed creative theories or exhibited judicial creativity.[56]

Ripoff Report

The foregoing cases happened following the dot.com implosion of 2000-2001, giving Silicon Valley a boost.[57]

Global Royalties, Ltd. v Xcentric Ventures, LLC[58] describes its situation by saying the following:

> This is a defamation action. Plaintiffs ("Global") broker investments in gemstones. Defendants operate a website called Ripoff Report (www.ripoffreport. com), where

Cyber-Torts
Page 59

visitors are invited to post consumer complaints. On March 27, 2006, Ripoff Report visitor Spencer Sullivan, who is not a party to this action, posted a message on the site referring to Global's operation as a "scam." .... The amended complaint alleges that consumers who post on defendants' site "must answer several questions created and developed by [defendants]." .... The complaint gives only one example: When posting on defendants' site, consumers are required to chose a "category" with which to label their message. For the first statement, Sullivan chose "Con Artists" from a list.... Further, plaintiffs allege that defendants encourage defamatory postings in order to use them as leverage "to coerce businesses and individuals to pay for [defendants'] Corporate Advocacy Program, which purports to provide assistance in investigating and resolving the posted complaints."....

Sullivan posted a second entry on June 8, 2006, which he said was in response to a threat of legal action from plaintiffs' counsel.... Sullivan wrote that he was not aware of any bad business practices on the part of Global itself, but that two individuals "involved with" Global had treated him dishonorably and had engaged in criminal acts.... Sullivan added that anyone looking to invest in gemstones should first call the Royal Canadian Mounted Police, Commercial Crime Unit.

Sullivan posted a third and final entry about Global on June 16, 2006. He again claimed that he had been "threatened" by plaintiffs' counsel, who advised him to discontinue the postings.... His message ends, "I think that any upstanding commercial operation could bear the scrutiny of a crime unit without any issue." ... At some point, Sullivan allegedly contacted defendants and asked that his entries be removed from the website, but defendants refused.

The Court granted Defendant's motion to dismiss. The owner of Ripoff Reports is named

Cyber-Torts
Page 61

Ed Magedson. Apparently, somebody burned down one of Mr. Magedson's houses. Too bad the dispute couldn't have been resolved with civil litigation. Ed Magedson also talks about the hundreds of threat letters that he has received, and the Russian hackers who attack Ripoff Report.[59]

The Ripoff Report home page, www.ripoffreport.com, encourages posting rants. Not coincidentally, they also peddle their "V.I.P. Arbitration" service and make money thereby. They have a policy of never removing a post (although they do allow making additional comments to report developments).

Ripoff Report didn't win them all, though. For example,

- *MCW, Inc. v. badbusinessbureau.com(RipOff Report/Ed Magedson/XCENTRIC Ventures LLC)* 2004 WL 833595, No. Civ.A.3:02-CV-2727-G (N.D. Tex. April 19, 2004).[82]

The court **rejected** the defendant's motion to dismiss on the grounds of Section 230 immunity, ruling that the plaintiff's allegations that the defendants wrote disparaging report titles and headings, and themselves wrote disparaging editorial messages about the plaintiff, rendered them information. The Web site, www.badbusinessbureau.com, allows users to upload "reports" containing complaints about businesses they have dealt with.

- *Hy Cite Corp. v. badbusinessbureau.com (RipOff Report/Ed Magedson/XCENTRIC Ventures LLC)*, 418 F. Supp. 2d 1142 (D. Ariz. 2005).[83]

The court **rejected** immunity and found the defendant was an "information content provider" under Section 230 using much of the same reasoning as the *MCW* case.

https://www.courtlistener.com/opinion/25 00235/hy-cite-corp-v-badbusinessbureau-com-llc/

Zango, Inc. v. Kaspersky Lab, Inc.[60]

In 2009, Zango alleged Kaspersky anti-malware blocked Zango unjustly. The court dismissed the claim pursuant to §230. The court did not hold in *Zango* that the immunity of §230 was limitless. The court noted how, as a complement to Section 230(c)(1)'s rule that websites are not liable for third-party content, Section 230(c)(2) says that online services are not liable for blocking or removing third-party content. Defendants prefer to rely on Section 230(c)(1) instead because, among other things, Section 230(c)(2) requires that blocking and removal decisions be made "in good faith." Plaintiffs *always* have incentives to contest the defendant's good faith, which delays the court's application of Section 230(c)(2)'s immunity-and sometimes overcomes it. The case is an example where the 9th Circuit used Section 230(c)(2) to provide wide-ranging protection for vendors of antispam, anti-virus, and anti-malware services.

The *Zango* ruling is said to be the main reason why we rarely see lawsuits anymore against those service providers for their blocking or removal decisions.[61]

Blockowicz v. Williams[62]

David, Mary, and Lisa Blockowicz received an injunction ordering Joseph David Williams and Michelle Ramey to remove defamatory comments they posted about the Blockowiczs on www. ripoffreport.com, among other websites. Williams and Ramey never responded to the injunction, prompting the Blockowiczs to contact the websites on which the statements were posted to secure compliance with the injunction. Every website complied, except for RipoffReport. The Blockowiczs asked the district court that issued the injunction to enforce it against Xcentric Ventures, LLC, ("Xcentric") the host of RipoffReport, and Ed Magedson, the website's manager, pursuant to F.R.C.P. 65(d)(2)(C). The district court declined, and the Blockowiczs appealed the district court's decision. They argued that Xcentric and Magedson fit within Rule 65, and thus should be bound by the injunction, because they had "actual notice" of the injunction, and they were "in active concert or participation" with the defendants in violating the injunction by failing to remove the defamatory statements. The Seventh Circuit affirmed, saying Xcentric and Magedson were not "in active concert or participation" with the defendants pursuant to Rule 65(d)(2)(C).

Doe v. MySpace[63]

In *Doe v. MySpace*, in the summer of 2005, at age thirteen, Julie Doe ("Julie") lied about her age, represented that she was eighteen years old, and created a profile on MySpace.com. Her action allowed her to circumvent all safety features of the Web site and resulted in her profile being made public. Nineteen-year-old Pete Solis was able to initiate contact with Julie in April 2006 when she was fourteen. The two communicated offline on several occasions after Julie provided her telephone number. They met in person in May 2006, and, at this meeting, Solis sexually assaulted Julie.

The Court held that CDA § 230 barred a negligence claim against MySpace.

Cyberbullying Led to Megan Meier's Suicide

Another abuse of MySpace occurred in 2009 when Lori Drew, 50, was accused of participating in a cyberbullying scheme against 13-year-old Megan Meier who later committed suicide. Prosecutors said Drew conspired to create a fake MySpace account for "Josh Evans" with her then 13-year-old daughter, Sarah, and a then-18-year-old employee and family friend named Ashley Grills.

Prosecutors alleged that Drew and the two others used the profile to lure Megan Meier into an online relationship with "Josh" to find out what Megan was saying about Drew's daughter online. But in October, one of the group, writing as Josh, turned against Megan, and told her that the world would be a better place without her. Shortly afterward, Megan hanged herself in her bedroom.

The judge overturned the guilty verdicts against Lori Drew, issuing a directed acquittal on three misdemeanor charges.[64]

Jones v. Dirty World Entertainment Recordings LLC[65,66]

Sarah Jones was the target of postings on the "DirtyWorld" website casting doubt upon Jones' chastity. Ms. Jones was a schoolteacher and a member of the Ben-gals cheerleader squad (for the Cincinnati Bengals football team). Ms. Jones was a victim of defamation *per se*, but Section 230 immunized the culprit, a website called "Dirty World".

Dirty.com is a site devoted to spreading gossip, often about college students. The site's founder, Nik Richie, has encouraged readers to email him "dirt" on people they know. Richie pastes his favorite emails in blog posts, often alongside images showing ordinary people "scantily clad, inebriated, and unfaithful." Posts have led to a torrent of abuse, with commenters accusing the subjects of "dirt" of having sexually transmitted infections, psychiatric disorders, and financial problems.... Richie has admittedly "ruined people sometimes out of fun...." That admission is not against interest—he knows well that he cannot be sued for his role in the abuse because what users do is on them. Courts applying section 230's immunity provision have dismissed efforts to hold Richie responsible for defamatory posts that have damaged lives and careers....

Jones sued on allegations of defamation, libel *per se*, false light, and intentional inflection of emotional distress. After Jones won a substantial jury verdict, the 6th Circuit reversed, saying Section 230 barred the suit. The Court adopted the "material contribution" test to determine whether a website operator is responsible, in whole or in part, for the creation or development of tortious information.

The site should not have been protected from liability since it was designed for the express purpose of hosting defamation and privacy invasions. Immunizing it turned the notion of the Good Samaritan on its head since its interests were aligned with the abusers. Enjoying §230 immunity was a windfall for the site operator who gave lip service to preventing defamation in the site's terms of service but encouraged his "Dirty Army" to email him "dirt" and chose which gossip to post.

The Dirty's Legal FAQs page[67] was extremely smug in its proclamation that the law does not permit anybody to sue the platform owner.[68],[69],[70],[71],[72]

Kimzey v. Yelp! Inc.[73]

Kimzey filed a *pro se* complaint in the district court alleging that Yelp was liable for the reviews by Sarah K under the Racketeer Influenced and Corrupt Organizations Act ("RICO"), 18 U.S.C. § 1964(c); the Washington Consumer Protection Act, Wash. Rev. Code § 19.86.020; and Washington's libel law. Specifically, the complaint alleged that Yelp "caused to appear a Libelous Per Se statement ... on ... Google." By "caused to appear," Kimzey seemed to assert that Yelp found the review on another website and posted it as a comment on its own website. Kimzey asserted that Yelp went on to publish the statements by Sarah K as "advertisements" or as a "promotion" on Google as part of a "Traffic Acquisition" program. After clicking on the "promotion," a Google user would be "directed to Yelp.com and then shown Yelp sponsored [sic] advertising." At the center of this allegedly creative process was a star rating, which Kimzey alleged "Yelp has developed and created" by "design[ing] the star image and creat[ing] the color."

Kimzey also alleged that the content of at least the first review posted by Sarah K bore the indicia of an "illegal scheme ... operated by the EL-AD Group, which uses thousands of fictitious locksmith business names on the Internet in every major US city, to promote themselves." The connection between Yelp and this claimed scheme was not clearly articulated in the complaint: Kimzey alleged that ELAD's purported statement "transitioned to Yelp.com and was linked to the Plaintiffs [sic] business name" where it then "transitioned to Google.com as a Yelp promotion."

The Court characterized Kimzey's pleading as "far from lucid and the opening brief cryptic to the point of opacity", the court proceeded to address and dismiss each claim. Creative pleading did not accomplish any progress.

America is Different

The First Amendment is unique to American law. The American fondness for Freedom of Speech and Freedom of the Press has always made suing for defamation in America a difficult proposition. With the *Sullivan*[74] and *Gertz*[75] cases, it became even more unlikely. Courts have considered several factors, including the status of the plaintiff as private individual or public figure, whether the statements were alleged to be facts or opinions, and whether the topic of discussion was a matter of legitimate public concern.

Another difficulty is the *Erie* doctrine,[76] the principle that State common law governs tort actions, even when a case is in Federal Court because of diversity jurisdiction. With the internet being not only a multi-State, but a multi-national phenomenon, the prospect of predicting what law a jurisdiction might find applicable becomes extremely complicated.

Section 230 is uniquely an American law. Some other countries provide a limited amount of protection for online intermediaries, few are as firm or as sweeping as Section 230. The U.S. has an inclination toward nearly absolute free speech. That traces back to the nation's founding. At the time of the formation of the U.S. government, there was a concern that free speech and press are a necessary check on government power.[77]

To address the problem of libel tourism, the 111th Congress passed the SPEECH Act (Securing the Protection of our Enduring and Established Constitutional Heritage Act)[78], making foreign libel judgments unenforceable in U.S. courts, unless those judgments are compliant with the U.S. First Amendment. President Barack Obama signed the act into law.

EU "Right to Be Forgotten"

The potentially permanent nature of postings to the internet is an area of proper concern. In the European Union, the General Data Protection Regulation (GDPR) governs how personal data must be collected, processed, and erased.[79] The "right to be forgotten," which received a lot of press after the 2014 judgment from the EU Court of Justice, set the precedent for the right of erasure provision contained in the GDPR. GDPR gives individuals the right to ask organizations to delete their personal data, but organizations don't always have to do it.

In May 2014, Google complied with the European Union's ruling enabling citizens to request to have certain URLs removed from search results.[80] A year and a half later (in its bi-annual Transparency Report) Google announced it received 348,085 such requests, the bulk of them coming from France and Germany, followed by the UK, Spain and Italy.

§ 230 Begins to Weaken

Section 230's first decade was marked by a rapid expansion of immunity for websites. The second decade saw a gradual—but real—erosion of Section 230 immunity.[81] Several cases began to appear showing that the immunity of Section 230 is not absolute.

In 2001 and 2002, U.S. courts issued written opinions in at least ten cases in which online intermediaries claimed Section 230 immunity. Of the ten cases, the courts concluded that eight intermediaries were immune. The remaining two cases involved intellectual property claims (which are explicitly exempt from Section 230).[82]

In contrast, between July 1, 2015, and June 30, 2016, in fourteen of twenty-seven cases, the courts refused to provide intermediaries with full immunity.[83] The courts' refusals to immunize the sites stemmed largely from two theories:

(1) the Roommates.com / Accusearch rationale that the sites somehow contributed to the illegal content, and

(2) the Barnes/Internet Brands argument that the sites were sued for activities other than publishing and

speaking. Four landmark cases from the second decade involved victims.[84]

Of particular hope is the holding that a claim for promissory estoppel may succeed where a negligence claim did not.[85]

Section 230 does not have to be a hall pass, a get-out-of-jail free card for anything to do with the internet. in the Ninth Circuit, Section 230 does not protect websites from lawsuits arising from their failure to warn.[86]

Negligence is still negligence, even if it is Jack Dorsey who was negligent. Criminal fraud is still criminal fraud, even if it is Jack Dorsey who committed the crime.

Fair Housing Council of San Fernando Valley v. Roommates.com[87]

The surge of enthusiasm for the bright, shiny, new Internet began to wane a little with the *roommates.com* case. In the *roommates.com* case, the 9th Circuit plumbed the depths of the immunity provided by section 230. The Plaintiffs alleged the Defendant website had violated certain fair housing laws with particular questions regarding race, religion, etc. The 9th Circuit found Section 230 would not shield a website that asked specifically illegal questions. Roommates.com had participated in the development and creation of content to the extent of removing them from the immunity of Section 230. (The website in *Carafano* had, in contrast, used relatively neutral tools.) There was mention of inter-circuit conflict, which might have been a ticket to the U. S. Supreme Court. Currently, there appears to have been no U. S. Supreme Court opinions clarifying the proper extent of Section 230 immunity.

Oddly, after nearly a decade of litigation, the third time the case came to the 9th Circuit, the Court decided that the housing discrimination laws didn't apply to roommate situations.[88] One can argue that the language in *roommates.com* is *dicta*.

Judge Kozinski made his distaste for Internet exceptionalism clear in the Roommates.com opinion.

> It is a mistake to fall into [the] trap of believing that the set of human interactions that is conducted online can be neatly grouped together into a discrete "cyberspace" that operates under its own rules. Technological innovations give us new capabilities, but they don't change the fundamental ways that humans deal with each other….[W]hen the internet is

involved in a controversy only because the parties happened to use it to communicate, new legal rules will rarely be necessary. When the substance of the offense is that something was communicated, then the harm occurs regardless of the tools used to communicate....[T]he vast majority of internet cases that have reached the courts have not required new legal rules to solve them.

The phenomenal growth of the tech sector has taken them out of the condition of needing baby crib and playpen protection. In fact, big tech companies have gotten so big, ordinary people are the ones who need protection from big tech.

The Internet is no longer a fragile new means of communication that could easily be smothered in the cradle by overzealous enforcement of laws and regulations applicable to brick-and-mortar businesses. Rather, it has become a dominant—perhaps the preeminent—means through which commerce is conducted.

And its vast reach into the lives of millions is exactly why we must be careful not to exceed the scope of the immunity provided by Congress and thus give online businesses an unfair advantage over their real-world counterparts, which must comply with laws of general applicability.

Roommates @ 1164.

"[T]he Internet has outgrown its swaddling clothes and no longer needs to be so gently coddled."[89]

Although its online forms asked arguably discriminatory questions, Roommates.com was ultimately found not liable because the anti-discrimination laws were not applicable to roommate housing situations.[90]

FTC v. Accusearch[91]

Accusearch paid its researchers to acquire telephone records, knowing that the confidentiality of the records was protected by law. It contributed mightily to the unlawful conduct of its researchers. The company proceeded to sell people's phone records illegally. The court found Accusearch did not have §230 immunity.

Trial Court Proceedings

The Federal Trade Commission (FTC) brought suit against the operator of the website, Accusearch Inc., and its president and owner, Jay Patel (collectively, Accusearch), to stop Accusearch's sale of confidential information and to require it to disgorge its profits from the sale of information contained in telephone records. The FTC alleged that Accusearch's trade in telephone records (which are protected from disclosure under § 702 of the Telecommunications Act of 1996 constituted an unfair practice in violation of Section 5(a) of the Federal Trade Commission Act (FTCA). The district court granted summary judgment to the FTC, and after further briefing entered an injunction restricting Accusearch's future trade in telephone records and other personal information.

Appellate Court Proceedings

On appeal, Accusearch contended that (1) the FTC's unfair trade practices claim should have been dismissed because Accusearch broke no law and because the FTC had no authority to enforce the Telecommunications Act; (2) it was immunized from suit by the protections provided to websites by Section 230 of the Communications Decency Act of 1996; and (3) the injunction was unnecessary to prevent it from resuming trade in telephone records and was unconstitutionally overbroad.

The appellate court affirmed. First, the court held that conduct may constitute an unfair practice under §5(a) of the FTCA even if it is not otherwise unlawful, and the FTC may pursue an unfair practice even if the practice is facilitated by violations of a law not administered by the FTC, such as the Telecommunications Act. Second, Accusearch's claimed defense under the CDA fails because it acted as an "information content provider" (and thus is not entitled to immunity) with respect to the information that subjected it to liability under the FTCA. Finally, the injunction was proper despite Accusearch's prior halt to its unfair practices and the possibility that the resumption of those practices would be criminally prosecuted; and Accusearch waived in district court its claim on appeal that the injunction was overbroad.

Barnes v. Yahoo!, Inc.[92]

The *Barnes v. Yahoo!* case stemmed from a dangerous, cruel, and highly indecent use of the internet for the apparent purpose of revenge. In late 2004, Cecilia Barnes broke off a lengthy relationship with a boyfriend. For reasons that are unclear, he responded by posting profiles of Barnes on a website run by Yahoo!, Inc. ("Yahoo").

The profiles contained nude photographs of Barnes and her boyfriend, taken without her knowledge. Barnes did not authorize her former boyfriend to post the profiles. The profiles also contained open solicitation whether express or implied to engage in sexual intercourse. The ex-boyfriend proceeded to conduct discussions in Yahoo's online "chat rooms," posing as Barnes, and directing correspondents to the fraudulent profiles. The profiles also included the addresses and telephone number at Barnes' place of employment. Before long, men whom Barnes did not previously know were peppering the office with emails, phone calls, and personal visits, all in the expectation of sex.

Barnes attempted to have the profile removed. In accordance with instructions from Yahoo policy, Barnes mailed a copy of her photo ID and a signed statement denying her involvement with the profiles and requesting their removal. After a month, Yahoo had failed to respond. The undesired advances from unknown men continued. Barnes asked Yahoo again by mail to remove the profiles. Nothing happened. The next month, Barnes sent Yahoo two more mailings. At the same time, a local news program was preparing to broadcast a report on the incident. The day before the initial air date of the broadcast, Yahoo responded. Its Director of Communications, a Ms. Osako, called Barnes and asked her to directly fax the previous statements she had mailed. Ms. Osako told Barnes she would "personally walk the statements over to the division responsible for stopping unauthorized profiles and they would take care of it." Barnes relied on Ms. Osako's statement and took no further action at that time regarding the profiles and the trouble they had caused. About two months passed without word from Yahoo, so Barnes filed a lawsuit in Oregon state court. Shortly thereafter, the profiles disappeared from Yahoo's website, apparently never to return.

Barnes' complaint against Yahoo alleged two causes of action under Oregon law. First, the complaint alleged a tort for the negligent provision or non-provision of services which Yahoo undertook to provide, citing section 323 of the Restatement (Second) of Torts (1965), which described the elements of the claim. The court referred to the tort as a "negligent undertaking." Barnes also referred in her complaint and in her briefs to Yahoo's "promise" to remove the indecent profiles and her reliance thereon to her detriment. The court construed such references to allege a cause of action under section 90 of the Restatement (Second) of Contracts (1981).

The court noted how a provider of information services might get sued for violating anti-discrimination laws, see, *e.g.*, *Roommates*, 521 F.3d 1157; for fraud, negligent misrepresentation, and ordinary negligence, see, e.g., *Doe v. MySpace, Inc.*, 528 F.3d 413 (5th Cir. 2008), *cert. denied*, 129 S. Ct. 600; for false light, see, *e.g.*, *Flowers v. Carville*, 310 F .3d 1118 (9th Cir. 2002); or even for negligent publication of advertisements that cause harm to third parties, see *Braun v. Soldier of Fortune Magazine, Inc.*, 968 F.2d 1110 (11th Cir. 1992).

Defamation law sometimes imposes "an affirmative duty to remove a publication made by another." Prosser and Keaton on Torts § 113, at 803. Courts have applied this principle, including in a case that reads like a low-tech version of the *Barnes* case. In *Hellar v. Bianco*, 244 P.2d 757 (Cal. Ct. App. 1952)[93], a woman received a phone call from a man who sought to arrange an unconventional, but apparently amorous, liaison. *Id.* at 758. After being rebuffed, the man informed the woman that her phone number appeared on the bathroom wall of a local bar along with writing indicating that she "was an unchaste woman who indulged in illicit amatory ventures." *Id.* The woman's husband promptly called the bartender and demanded he remove the defamatory graffiti, which the bar-tender said he would do when he got around to it.

Shortly thereafter, the husband marched to the bar, policeman in tow, and discovered the offending scrawl still gracing the wall. *Id.* at 759.

He defended his wife's honor by suing the bar's owner.

The California Court of Appeal held that it was "a question for the jury whether, after knowledge of its existence, the bar owner negligently allowed the defamatory matter to remain for so long a time as to be chargeable with its republication."

The *Barnes* Court ruled that there may have been a cause of action pursuant to the doctrine of promissory estoppel for breach of contract and that Section 230(c)(1) did not preclude such an action.

Writing for the panel, Judge O'Scannlain observed Barnes did not seek to hold Yahoo liable as a publisher or speaker of third-party content, but rather as the counter-party to a contract, as a promisor who has breached.[94]

Doe v. Internet Brands[95,96]

Online predators had committed crimes by using a website called "Model Mayhem" to lure women into being drugged and raped.[97] One of their victims ("Doe") sued Internet Brands, the company that owned the website, alleging they knew about the rapists but did not warn her or the website's other users. She filed an action against Internet Brands alleging liability for negligence under California law based on that failure to warn.

The 9th Circuit held the failure to warn claim was not barred by Section 230 immunity.

Doe v Internet Brands and many other similar cases demonstrate a gradual willingness of courts to seek to hold intermediaries accountable for third-party content where the intermediaries encouraged or somehow augmented the third-party content. Section 230 does not continue to act as a complete bar to relief for plaintiffs who believe that they have been wronged online, but it still puts a thumb on the scales in favor of Big Tech.[98]

Secondary liability should not reach every company that plays any hand in assisting the online wrongdoer, of course. Before secondary liability attaches, the plaintiff should have to show that the defendant provided a crucial service, knew of the illegal or actionable activity, and had a right and a cost-justified ability to control the infringer's actions.

Such an argument is consistent with traditional tort principles (as well as Judge Kozinski's dissent in Perfect 10 v. Visa regarding copyright liability). 47 USC 230's immunity has been interpreted as breaking venerable principles. Bright judges imbued in the common law can have a tough time with Congress' rejection of traditional tort principles (as well as the concomitant reduction in judicial discretion).

Another example is *Diamond Ranch Academy v Filer*[99], where a residential treatment facility filed a defamation lawsuit against the operator of a website that allowed former facility websites to share their stories. The website operator moved to dismiss the lawsuit under Section 230, asserting that she merely summarized and made editorial changes to some of the content provided by third parties, just as the museum security group in *Batzel*. The district court rejected the argument, concluding that the posts on her website "do not lead a person to believe that she is quoting a third party."[100]

The future should have a balance between privacy and free speech. Beyond its infancy, the internet may also be progressing beyond its adolescence. The world-wide audience is at everybody's fingertips. Paper medium often had a valuable premium on limited space. Broadcasting had limited frequencies. The internet has relatively unlimited potential.

It may seem surprising that a revenge pornographer, a gossip-site curator, and a platform pairing predators with young people in one-on-one chats have something in common.

Yet they have been granted blanket immunity from liability by lower courts' interpretations of § 230 of the CDA beyond what the text, context, and purpose support. The CDA was part of a campaign (rather ironically in retrospect) to restrict access to sexually explicit material online. Lawmakers wanted to devise a safe harbor for online providers engaged in self-regulation. The CDA's origins in the censorship of "offensive" material are inconsistent with overly broad interpretations that have served to immunize from liability platforms dedicated to abuse and or those that deliberately tolerate illegality.

§ 230 immunity may well be too sweeping. In a brick and mortar space, a business that arranged private rooms for strangers to meet knowing that sexual predators were using its service to meet kids would have to do a great deal more than warn people to proceed "at their own peril" to avoid liability when bad things happened. A physical magazine devoted to publishing user-submitted malicious gossip about non-public figures would face a blizzard of lawsuits as false and privacy-invading materials harmed people's lives. And a company that knowingly allowed designated foreign terrorist groups to use their physical services would face all sorts of lawsuits from victims of terrorist attacks. Something is out of whack—and requires rethinking—when such activities are categorically immunized from liability merely because they happen online....

This was not, as highlighted below, what Congress had in mind in 1996 when it adopted the Communications Decency Act (CDA). The CDA was part of a broad campaign—rather ironically in retrospect—to restrict access to sexually explicit material online. Lawmakers thought they were devising a limited safe harbor from liability for online providers engaged in self-regulation. Because regulators could not keep up with the volume of noxious material online, the participation of private actors was essential....

Section 230 is overdue for a rethinking. If courts do not construe the scope of federal immunity to avoid injustice, we argue, Congress should amend the law. This is not to discount the important role that the immunity provision has played over the past twenty years. Far from it. Section 230 immunity has enabled innovation and expression beyond the imagination of the operators of early bulletin boards and computer service providers the provision was designed to protect. But its overbroad interpretation has left victims of online abuse with no leverage against sites whose business model is abuse. This state of affairs can be changed without undermining free expression and innovation. Having broad protections for free speech and clear rules of the road is important for online platforms to operate with confidence. Section 230, at least as it is currently understood, is not necessary for either of these. With modest adjustments to section 230, either through judicial interpretation or legislation, we can have a robust culture of free speech online without shielding from liability platforms designed to host illegality or who deliberately host illegal content. [101]

Anybody can do a background check on anybody. Gossip and shaming, when translated to the internet, can take on some problematic dimensions. Between privacy and free speech, we often want both. The law must take a middle path.

J.S. v. Vill. Voice Media Holdings, LLC

In the 2015 case of *J.S. v. Vill. Voice Media Holdings, LLC*[102], the plaintiffs had been the repeated victims of horrific acts committed in the shadows of the law (children were bought and sold for sexual services online on Backpage.com). The Court found that although federal law shielded website operators from state law liability for merely hosting content developed by users, where defendants helped to produce the illegal content and therefore were subject to liability under state law. Justice Wiggins, in his concurring opinion, noted the following:

Recognizing that the statute contains competing policy goals, recent circuit court decisions have protected "Good Samaritan" and neutral behavior while asserting that culpable behavior by websites is not protected under section 230. Roommates.com, 521 F.3d at 1175 ("[t]he message to website operators is clear: If you don't encourage illegal content[ ] or design your website to require users to input illegal content," you will not be held liable for hosting third-party content). Courts specifically reject the subsection 230(c)(1) defense when the underlying cause of action does not treat the information content provider as a "publisher or speaker" of another's information. See, e.g., City of Chicago v. StubHub!, Inc., 624 F.3d 363, 366 (7th Cir. 2010) (subsection 230(c)(1) defense inapplicable because suit to collected city's amusement tax "does not depend on who 'publishes' any information or is a 'speaker'"). More analogous to the instant case, the Ninth Circuit recently permitted a lawsuit against an ISP on a theory of promissory estoppel. Barnes, 570 F.3d at 1106-09. These cases provide meaningful limitations on the defenses afforded by subsection 230(c)(1).

Giving ISPs free rein has resulted in some wonderful developments and in some horrible developments. Courts, in deciding cases on the ground, have to follow statutes unless they are unconstitutional, and have to follow case precedent (usually). There isn't time to re-invent the wheel and re-consider the possibly far-reaching, complicated issues about whether any particular wording in a statute is good or bad. Narrow issues of statutory interpretation are of a different magnitude than broad issues of evil versus good. It has to be up to Congress to change a line like § 230 when necessary.

Backpage's criminal acts subsequently resulted in several convictions. There appears to be no logical reason why crimes leading to convictions shouldn't also be accompanied by civil suits leading to financial remedies.

Anonymity and Identity

The Ku Klux Klan used white hoods and cloaks to conduct their heinous activities with anonymity. Wrongdoers on the internet treasure their anonymity just as much.

Alcoholics like to remain anonymous.[103] Concealing their identities is crucial to the strategy of confessing their misdeeds to make themselves feel better while escaping any actual accountability.

Before jurisdiction even comes into play, it's necessary to discover where - and who - the wrongdoer is before you can think about suing.[104] The problem is there are so many ways to hide one's identity. There are numerous services that will mask a user's IP address by routing traffic through various servers, usually for a fee. This makes it difficult to track down the wrongdoer.

Internet "passports" for individuals and accreditation for businesses may help combat the problem. Some studies have shown that people are more likely to engage in offensive and/or illegal behavior online because of the perception of anonymity. However, attempts to better track online identity raise serious issues for privacy advocates and result in political backlash. An end to (or serious limitation of) anonymity on the Internet could have serious consequences in countries where the government punishes dissenters, so even if the technological challenge of identifying every online user could be overcome, many lawmakers would be hesitant to mandate it. Cyber-wrongdoers exploit the rights and privileges of a free society, including anonymity, to benefit themselves.

Jurisdictional issues still present a challenge, particularly when the wrongdoer is in another country, but more and more governmental entities are recognizing the harm that cyber-torts do to their citizens and are working together. Countries (and states within the U.S.) are cooperating to adopt consistent laws, and forming interjurisdictional task forces to deal with cybercrime that crosses state and national boundaries.

One prominent example, Facebook, requires users setting up profiles to register under their real names and to verify their identities by providing e-mail addresses.

In re Anonymous Online Speakers,[105] is a 2011 9th Circuit opinion with an excellent discussion about the competing interests of anonymity and identification. The proceeding was a short chapter in an acrimonious and long-running business dispute between Quixtar, Inc. ("Quixtar"), successor to the well-known Amway Corporation, and Signature Management TEAM, LLC ("TEAM"). Quixtar sued TEAM, claiming that TEAM orchestrated an Internet smear campaign via anonymous postings and videos disparaging Quixtar and its business practices. As part of the discovery process, Quixtar sought testimony from a TEAM employee regarding the identity of five anonymous online speakers who made defamatory comments about Quixtar. The employee refused to identify the anonymous speakers on First Amendment grounds. The Court noted how the factors to consider can include the importance of the speech (*i.e.* political versus commercial).

In 2011, President Obama was inquiring about a National Strategy for Trusted Identities in Cyberspace.[106] Further investigation into that line may be appropriate.

Posters are often much braver online than they are in person.[107] Anonymity frees people to defy social norms. When individuals believe, rightly or wrongly, that their acts won't be attributed to them personally, they become less concerned about social conventions. Research has shown that people tend to ignore social norms when they are hidden in a group or behind a mask. Social psychologists call this condition deindividuation. People are more likely to act destructively if they do not perceive the threat of external sanction. Anonymity is often associated with violence, vandalism, and stealing. This is true of adults and children. People are more inclined to act on prejudices when they think they cannot be identified.

A classic study conducted by the social psychologist Phillip Zimbardo involved female college students who believed they were delivering a series of painful electric shocks to two women.[108] Half of the students wore hoods and oversized lab coats, their names replaced by numbers; the other half received nametags that made it easy to identify them. The study found that the anonymous students delivered twice as much electric shock to subjects as the non-anonymous students. The anonymous students increased the shock time over the course of the trials and held down their fingers even longer when the subjects twisted and moaned before them. That the students ignored the pain of those affected by their actions showed the dramatic change in their mentality and empathy when they were anonymous.

Cyber-Terrorism

Fields v. Twitter[109]

Lloyd "Carl" Fields, Jr., and James Damon Creach were killed while working as government contractors in Jordan. ISIS claimed credit for the attack. Plaintiffs-Appellants sued Defendant-Appellee Twitter, Inc. (Twitter) pursuant to 18 U.S.C. § 2333(a), the civil remedies provision of the Anti-Terrorism Act (ATA), alleging that they were injured "by reason of" Twitter's knowing provision of material support to ISIS. Twitter moved to dismiss the case, and its motion was granted. The district court held that Plaintiffs-Appellants had failed to plead that they were injured "by reason of" Twitter's conduct. The district court also ruled that Twitter's liability was precluded by § 230 of the Communications Decency Act (CDA), 47 U.S.C. §230(b), because Plaintiffs-Appellants' claims sought to treat Twitter as the publisher of ISIS's content. Plaintiffs-Appellants appealed both holdings. The Ninth Circuit affirmed on the ground that Plaintiffs-Appellants failed to adequately plead proximate causation.

Depending on the circumstance, the failure to remove specific ISIL accounts might be understood as negligent or reckless conduct falling within the safe harbor immunity. Given the scale of Twitter's user base (in the hundreds of millions), Twitter should be immunized from liability for failing to remove accounts about which it had not been notified or for removing accounts after a normal review process. The platform is currently engaged in good-faith screening efforts. In the first six months of 2017, the platform removed more than 377,000 pro-terrorism accounts. Sustained failure to remove an account despite repeated notifications, by contrast, might well strip the company of immunity in a specific case. Note that this would not in and of itself give rise to liability. Instead, it would merely require that Twitter defend a suit on its merits rather than being automatically shielded from answering claims asserted against it.[110]

We should be skeptical that Section 230, as currently interpreted, is really optimizing free speech. It gives an irrational degree of free speech benefit to harassers and scofflaws, but ignores important free speech costs to victims. Individuals have difficulty expressing themselves in the face of online assaults. They shut down their blogs, sites, and social network profiles not because they tire of them, but because continuing them provokes their attackers. Civil liberties organization Electronic Frontier Foundation has recognized that cyber harassment is "profoundly damaging to the free speech and privacy rights of the people targeted."[111]

Going forward the problem for the major social media sites like Twitter is not going to be removing too little extremist speech but rather removing too much in the face of threatened regulation by the EU Commission and EU member states.[112]

Cyber-Warfare

Cyber-Torts
Page 96

The large nations of the world have been preparing for cyber-war for some time,[113] both in terms of offensive and defensive strategies. Perhaps you've heard of the Great Firewall of China? An awareness of the potential and reality of the internet as a weapon of war should inform any discussion about civil litigation for online wrongdoing.

Cyber-Warfare has the potential to cause more destruction than any previously known weapon. What if cyber-warriors caused an enemy's electrical grids to fail? What if warring nations caused each other's essential computer systems to cease to function, disabling transportation, communication, and industry? What if computer hackers took control of the computerized financial world?

The effects, obviously, would be catastrophic beyond description. It is very important for the U.S.A. to prepare for the national defense needs of the future.

The reason there has been relatively little cyber-war thus far is the same reason no nation has used a nuclear weapon for war since 1945. So far, world leaders have recognized the costs of a destruction-retaliation cycle are too terrible and the benefits of diplomacy and cooperation are much preferable. The best defense against the potential disaster of cyber-war is for our political leaders to act with sufficient diplomacy, intelligence, tact, and wisdom to avoid a tragic scenario of cyber-war. So, to accomplish that, we should vote for sane, competent, civilized candidates.

Cyber-Crime and Cyber-Tort

It is important to distinguish between (1) crimes, (2) torts, and (3) things that are disgusting but neither crimes nor torts. Categories (1) and (2) are not entirely mutually exclusive. Violation of a criminal statute or other ordinance or rule may often be considered as evidence of negligence or intent for purposes of a civil tort suit.[114]

Varian Med. Sys. v. Delfino[115]

The judgment in *Varian Med. Sys. v. Delfino* gave plaintiffs $ 775,000 in damages. It was essentially upheld on appeal. The Defendants posted more than 13,000 derogatory messages online about the Plaintiffs. The Defendants also vowed to continue the posting of such messages till their death.

The Defendants' argument about Freedom of Speech was not effective. In particular, the court noted that even if exchanges online were typically freewheeling and irreverent, they were not exempt from established legal and social norms, and the "internet may be the new marketplace of ideas, ... but it can never achieve its potential as such unless it is subject to the civilizing influence of the law like all other social discourse".

Scheff v. Bock[116]

In 2006 a woman in Florida sued for internet defamation and won an $11.3M judgment by default.[117] The judgment was almost certainly uncollectable because the defendant did not have extraordinary assets.[118]

Revenge porn statutes

After a breakup, raw feelings have been known to set off a desire for revenge. Some jilted lovers have taken to posting intimate pictures of a former partner on the Internet. It's a phenomenon known as "revenge porn," and most States have enacted laws making it a crime.[119]

There has been a movement toward getting legislation passed against nonconsensual pornography. In 2013, there were three states that had such laws on the books and as of 2019, there were 46.[120]

The new law was a victory to Holly Jacobs, who was a victim of revenge porn. Jacobs went through what sounds like a typical boy-meets-girl story of falling in and out of love. The first year of the relationship, Jacobs and her partner lived in the same city, but she left to go to graduate school in Miami.[121] Ms. Jacobs continues:

> ...Facebook, Twitter, Google, Microsoft, Apple and Snapchat, and many of them have developed their own codes of conduct against the posting of the material and they don't allow it on their platforms.
>
> But those who do allow it, they hide behind what's called Communications Decency Act [Section] 230, which protects these sites from what third parties may post to their platform.
>
> It was written back in the time when the internet was just created and it was written to protect the platforms from having to chase after anything and everything and check on everything that anyone posted to their profile.

But they should still have some responsibility in policing it and to being able to catch it before it goes viral.

Now they've developed certain tools; Facebook actually has photo DNA technology that helps them to prevent the material from being posted to their site, so victims can actually reach out proactively if they suspect that this material may be posted. It's looking much more promising than it was when I first got to this area.

Washington State's legislature has also passed a law against non-consensual disclosure of intimate images.[122]

Doe v. Backpage[123]

In 2016 *Jane Doe No. 1 v. Backpage.com*, sex trafficking victims sued Backpage—a classifieds hub allegedly hosting "80 percent of the online advertising for illegal commercial sex in the United States."[124] The plaintiffs alleged Backpage did not have section 230 immunity for their sexual assault because it had deliberately structured its service to enable sex trafficking. Evidence showed that defendant had selectively removed postings discouraging sex trafficking and tailored its rules to protect the practice from detection, including allowing anonymized email and photographs stripped of metadata. Nonetheless, the court held that Backpage enjoyed immunity from liability, even as it recognized that plaintiffs' evidence was "persuasive."

The court reasoned that, "[s]howing that a website operates through a meretricious business model is not enough to strip away those protections." Neither the text of the statute nor its history required sweeping immunity from liability for sites like Backpage. It was part of the Communications Decency Act. Section 230 of the CDA was not meant to immunize services whose business was the active subversion of online decency—businesses that were not merely failing to take "Good Samaritan" steps to protect users from online indecency but are actually being Bad Samaritans. Granting immunity to platforms designed in part or in whole for illegal activity would have seemed absurd to the CDA's drafters.

The free expression calculus devised by the law's supporters often fails to consider the loss of voices in the wake of destructive harassment encouraged or tolerated by platforms. The many benefits the immunity has enabled could have been secured at a slightly lesser price.

Uber drivers have to have insurance, so if your Uber driver causes a collision and hurts you, the insurance will pay. Insurance cannot cover intentional acts, though, for obvious reasons. It would make sense if internet platforms had to have insurance to pay for their negligence, if proven, about torts committed through them.

Platform companies may not be selling the service, product, or content. They are instead selling matching algorithms, access to software, and a digital system of reputation and trust between users.

It is fine when the law can aid innovation, but as circumstance change, it is necessary to re-balance the scales of justice. Often regulatory controls are a matter of legitimate social tradeoffs and an emphasis on certain values. Section 230 amounts to a government subsidy benefiting platforms at the expense of injured people. Errors in regulation of technology are a great risk where the regulators don't understand the technology.

Platforms may need grievance mechanisms, insurance coverage, and compliance controls to comply with regulations. Such additions can also be good for business. There are many reasons that the Wild West of old had to be tamed to make it not so wild. Likewise, the internet needs more taming influence.

Uber and Lyft

Both Uber and Lyft are currently facing litigation in multiple states under the ADA.[125] In one case, an Uber driver allegedly placed a disabled passenger's service dog in the trunk, while other drivers are alleged to have sped past riders waiting in wheelchairs. As with its employment disputes, in these cases Uber argues that, because it is a technology company and not a transportation company, it does not fall under the purview of the ADA. Uber claims it cannot control the actions of its drivers who refuse to accept passengers with disabilities because the drivers are independent contractors, and thus, Uber has no legal obligation to ensure they comply with the ADA. Possibly in response to pending litigation, however, Uber launched its UberASSIST service to provide senior citizens and people with disabilities with specially trained drivers.[126]

The Kevin Bollaert case

Kevin Bollaert was charged under California law with Identity Theft and Extortion.[127] He had started a website called "ugotposted.com" that encouraged ex-boyfriends and husbands to post intimate pictures of their ex's along with contact information. When the women complained, he referred them to another of his websites called "ChangeMyReputation.com" and demand hundreds of dollars to remove the post. He was convicted on Feb. 2, 2015.[128] He was sentenced to eighteen years in prison.[129]

The charge of Identity Theft was criticized by legal analysts as being inapplicable to the facts.[130]

If the law can stop crime by website owners (Bollaert) and through website owners (Backpage.com), why stop there? Why not allow the rule of civil law to operate in cyberspace, too? It doesn't have to be the Wild West anymore.

The sheer volume of information flowing over the internet is unique in human experience.[131] In passing § 230, Congress may have had a glimpse of how unmanageable the internet might have become, and reasoned that providers had the best chance of regulating it.

Nonetheless, management and regulation are necessary in any civilized society.

The relatively recent cases pushing forward with bringing the rule of law (both criminal and civil) to the internet show that it is possible for courts to bring justice even where criminals and wrongdoers have used the internet to commit their heinous offenses.

Some speech may constitute a crime and a tort at the same time. The distinction between crime and tort is not always clear-cut, but it can be significant. Think of the O. J. Simpson criminal trial versus the civil suit. The different standard of proof can make a difference.

For further reading, see the excellent volume by Professor Danielle Keats Citron entitled "Hate Crimes in Cyberspace" published by the Harvard University Press in 2014.

First Amendment Arguments

The First Amendment to the U.S. Constitution is simple. The European description of the right to freedom of speech is more complicated.

Although cyber harassment contributes little to free speech values, regulation of it should comport with First Amendment doctrine. Speech shouldn't be censored merely because it is offensive or distasteful.

Ordinarily, laws purporting to restrict freedom of speech are often subject to "strict scrutiny review", which almost always means they will be found unconstitutional. There are exceptions, of course, the classic example being shouting "Fire!" in a crowded theatre. Where speech has obvious low value and the potential for harm greatly outweighs any possible contribution to the free flow of ideas, legal restrictions on speech are possible. Examples can include realistic threats, speech comprising criminal conduct, defamation, fraud, obscenity, and imminent and likely incitement of violence. In the context of the real world, First Amendment protections do not preclude actions for torts committed verbally.

The Ku Klux Klan may have freedom to say and do some things as expressions of their beliefs, but there are limits.[132] The process of regulating the legal and social consequences of individual internet use is still in development.

The Canadian Charter of Rights and Freedoms—Canada's equivalent of the U.S. Constitution's Bill of Rights—guarantees "fundamental freedoms," among them the "freedom of thought, belief, opinion and expression, including freedom of the press and other media of communication." But just above this guarantee is an important qualifier: these rights are "subject only to such reasonable limits prescribed by law as can be demonstrably justified in a free and democratic society."

There are several factors to consider in evaluating a potential First Amendment argument, including the following:

1.   The public importance of the issue versus the private nature of the speech;
2.   The status of the allegedly injured person as a public official, public figure, or private individual;
3.   The objectionability of the speech as being extremely offensive to an ordinary individual versus relatively unobjectionable;
4.   The extent of the propagation of the speech or communication – whether it was communicated to only a few people then retracted versus posted

online to four billion people now and all future generations forever.

In her book Consent of the Networked: The Worldwide Struggle for Internet Freedom, Rebecca MacKinnon argues that ISPs, search engines, and social media providers "have far too much power over citizens' lives, in ways that are insufficiently transparent or accountable to the public interest."[133]

The U.S.A. has an extraordinarily expansive view of free speech.[134] Our First Amendment free speech cases, like our right to own guns pursuant to the Second Amendment, is an example of exceptionalism in American law that can privilege the rights of actors over those of the acted upon.

In an interesting recent decision, the Second Circuit said the First Amendment does not permit a public official who utilizes a social media account for all manner of official purposes to exclude persons from an otherwise-open online dialogue because they expressed views with which the official disagrees.[135]

Another example of a defamation case involving blogging is the 2014 9th Circuit case of *Obsidian Finance v. Cox*[136] The defendant had posted allegedly defamatory statements on websites, one of which was named "obsidianfinancesucks.com" The Court applied the basic standards of defamation law. The jury had found in favor of plaintiffs, awarding the one $1.5 million and another $1 million in compensatory damages.

Public Forum Doctrine

The Public Forum doctrine says spaces the government has opened to the public for expressive activities may not be subject to content-based or viewpoint-based discrimination.[137] Some question whether the Public Forum Doctrine is coherent because rights of participants in a forum potentially clash with the speech rights of the private-forum owners themselves.[138]

Modern platforms of communication have turned out to be more powerful than governments in some situations.[139]

Twitter may own its servers, but the internet operates over publicly owned facilities. Much of the technology enabling the internet has been funded by the US Department of Defense. Some argue that the best response to disfavored speech on matters of public concern is more speech, not less.[140]

Part of the problem is there is no historical practice of the interactive space of a tweet being used for public speech and debate. Social media platforms represent a fundamental shift in how speech and civic engagement happens, and novel conflicts of speech rights can arise as a result. One particularly significant case held that a party violated the First Amendment rights of one of her constituents, when she banned him from a Facebook page she administered.[141]

Sometimes it is perfectly sensible to hold people liable for other people's speech. The print version of the New York Times may be liable for the speech of other people that it publishes, including that of its reporters, columnists, and even its advertisers. In fact, the famous case of *New York Times v. Sullivan* involved an advertisement that was the basis of Police Commissioner Sullivan's libel suit.[142] Similarly, book publishers are liable for the statements of authors they print.[143]

The most important decisions will not be made by courts construing the Constitution; they will be made by legislatures, administrative agencies, technologists, entrepreneurs, and end-users.

If you've never been the victim of slander, libel, and defamation of character, you might not appreciate how much it can hurt.

There have been some cases where judges have failed to comprehend how the innovations of new technology should have required the re-evaluation of established legal standards.

Insurance often covers situations where the insured was not at fault (i.e. PIP or UIM coverage), but the guilty party had neither insurance nor assets. It may be a very good idea to require providers of interactive computer services to obtain adequate insurance to pay for their negligence in facilitating the wrongdoing of users.

Internet Civil Rights Violations

Perhaps the most compelling argument for revoking § 230 is the way immune website owners can shield and facilitate hate speech. With proper regulation, the internet can be a powerful force for improvements in civil rights. Just look at Black Lives Matter and the protests against police violence in mid-2020 as an example. The cellphone video that captured the officer kneeling on George Floyd's neck spread across social media platforms — and it's the reason Americans learned about his controversial killing in the first place. Many of the cases of unconscionable use of force against black Americans have come to light as a result of videos posted to social media.

Civil rights violations have a dual character in that on one hand, they single out people from traditionally subordinated groups for abuse that wreaks special harm on victims and their communities and on the other hand, they explicitly or implicitly communicate a bigoted viewpoint.[144] The Supreme Court has rejected attempts to ban abusive expressions because their content may be more offensive to certain groups, but the First Amendment poses no obstacle to civil rights claims, including the ones at the heart of a cyber civil rights legal agenda, because they proscribe defendants' unequal treatment of individuals and the unique harm that such discrimination inflicts, not the offensive messages that harassers express.[145]

Chicago Lawyers' Committee for Civil Rights Under Law, Inc. v. Craigslist, Inc.[146]

In 2008, the Chicago Lawyers' Committee for Civil Rights Under Law, Inc. sued Craigslist for hosting users' discriminatory housing postings. Unlike the decision in *Roommates.com*, Craigslist was immune from liability for users' discriminatory housing postings because nothing in the service craigslist offered induced anyone to post any particular listing or express a preference for discrimination. The court rejected the claims that Craigslist caused the discriminatory posting just by hosting an interactive web forum. It also rejected the argument that discriminatory housing advertisements were an exception to CDA § 230.

2020 Controversy

Twitter recently added fact-check warnings to a pair of President Trump's tweets and on May 28, 2020 the President issued an executive order aimed at limiting the broad legal protections enjoyed by social media companies pursuant to §230, igniting a potentially far-reaching controversy.[147,148] The President's executive order directed investigation into reforms of §230, saying he was taking action to defend free speech from one of the gravest dangers it has faced in American history.[149]

Critical commentary followed.[150]

President Trump tweeted on May 29 that he wants to revoke Section 230.[151] On May 29, the president of the United States of America tweeted, simply, "REVOKE 230!" The message was all caps, with an exclamation mark for good measure.

On June 2, the Center for Democracy & Technology sued President Trump in the U.S. District Court for the District of Columbia, asking the court to declare the executive order of May 28, 2020 invalid.[152] Jerry Berman of the Center for Democracy & Technology had supported §230 at the time of its passage.

On June 9, four Republican senators sent an open letter to the FCC, urging chairman Ajit Pai to examine the "special status" afforded to social media sites under the statute.[153] The letter, authored by Marco Rubio, Kelly Loeffler, Kevin Cramer and Josh Hawley reads, in part:

> Social media companies have become involved in a range of editorial and promotional activity; like publishers, they monetize, edit, and otherwise editorialize user content. It is time to take a fresh look at Section 230 and to interpret the vague standard of "good faith" with specific guidelines and direction. In addition, it appears that courts have granted companies immunity for editing and altering content even though the text of Section 230 prohibits immunity for any content that the company "in part … develop[s]." These interpretations also deserve a fresh look. We therefore request that the FCC clearly define the framework under which technology firms, including social media companies, receive protections under Section 230.[154]

The letter adds that, unlike Trump, who currently has around 82 million followers, "everyday Americans" are "sidelined, silenced, or otherwise censored by these corporations." President Trump himself has had a longstanding problem with the rule, which he and fellow Republicans have accused of enabling the censorship of conservative free speech. While he's long been rumored to be interested in killing the legislation, Twitter's decision to issue a warning label on a Trump tweet appears to have been the final straw.

Pai reportedly voiced a disinterest in regulating social media sites in that manner previously.

Requesting that the Federal Communication Commission (FCC) take a fresh look at Section 230 of the Communications Decency Act and clearly define the criteria for which companies can receive protections under the statute is entirely reasonable. Recent troubling activities by social media companies, including partisan attempts to silence political speech and efforts to silence critics of the Chinese Communist Party, have shown the need for a re-examination of § 230.

Social media companies have become involved in a range of editorial and promotional activity; like publishers, they monetize, edit, and otherwise editorialize user content. It is time to take a fresh look at Section 230 and to interpret the vague standard of 'good faith' with specific guidelines and direction. Courts have granted companies immunity for editing and altering content even though the text of Section 230 prohibits immunity for any content that the company in part develops. The interpretations also deserve a fresh look. We should all be requesting that the FCC clearly define the framework under which technology firms, including social media companies, receive protections under Section 230.

Social media companies have not been living up to their obligations when they blur the lines between distributor and publisher by favoring one political point of view over another.

We should worry about everyday Americans who are sidelined, silenced, or otherwise censored by social media corporations. Social media companies, whose protections come from their acting as distributors, not publishers, have increasingly engaged in partisan editorializing, censorship of Chinese dissidents, and a host of politically motivated speech policing. While the actions speak for themselves, companies continue to enjoy Section 230 protections due to a lack of clear rules and judicial expansion of the statute.

As of June 17, 2020, the DOJ has recommended changes to §230 and congressmen have proposed new legislation.[155]

Civil Law on the Internet Will Not Kill It

Now that twenty years have passed, the question is whether the internet will die if Section 230 is no longer accorded a broad sweeping interpretation. Section 230's most fervent supporters argue that it is "responsible for the extraordinary Internet boom" and its evisceration would sound the death knell to innovation. To the extent the internet needed a broad liability shield when it was young, it certainly needs it no longer. Innovation on online platforms can coexist with an expectation that platform companies will behave according to some enforceable standard of conduct.

Let's put the apocalyptic rhetoric and fear mongering aside.[156] The internet doesn't belong to just Republicans, Democrats, big Silicon Valley tech companies, internet service providers, small Silicon Prairie start-ups, or the federal government. It belongs to everyone – it is global.

Arguments threatening the death of the internet may have emotional appeal, but they lack a rational basis. The technology of the internet intentionally makes it extremely robust. Nothing any individual, court, or nation can do will kill the internet. The internet will outlive all of us. That is a central feature of how scary it can be and how beautiful it can be. Postings on the internet may be there forever, shedding eternal shame or bringing eternal glory.

In contrast to a strike-oriented view of the CDA's safe harbor, its modest revision would not break the internet. Even if such concerns were founded at the time of its passage two decades ago, they are not today. Conditioning immunity from liability on reasonable efforts to address unlawful or wrongful activity would not end innovation or free expression. The current environment of perfect impunity for platforms deliberately facilitating online abuse is not a win for free speech because it allows harassers to speak unhindered while causing the harassed to withdraw from online interactions. With modest adjustments to §230, either through judicial interpretation or legislation, it is possible to have a robust culture of free speech online without shielding platforms from liability even when they are designed to host illegality or when they deliberately host illegal content.

The Future and Section 230

In enacting §230, Congress intended to encourage self-regulation on the internet. Self-regulation is often good, but it obviously fails when you are expecting self-regulation by criminals, liars, scoundrels, thieves, and hooligans. Then you need serious regulation, either by private companies, by government, or (preferably) by cooperation between the two.

Simply put, the evidence indicates that when platforms become content providers, they should no longer enjoy the §230 protections. There is also much to say in favor of legal provisions addressing issues of identification, notice, take-down, review, and put-back requirements. Big Tech can afford to be more responsible and accountable.

Some news websites, having received floods of complaints about nasty online comments underneath stories, have begun requiring users to post under their real name, via their Facebook logins. Complex, challenging, and severely damaging situations can require re-evaluation of the law. Section 230 needs a re-examination to address the systemic problems. It is possible to preserve the benefits of the internet while fixing its flaws.

Congress must take a hard look at Section 230's statutory subsidy for free speech.

Although there are well-meaning Yelp reviewers or Wikipedia-based amateur journalists, there are also trolls lurking in the background, ready to use free speech as a weapon.

It is unlikely all the evil will be rooted out of the internet, but platform owners can certainly start to bear a reasonable portion of the burden of improving the medium. The internet is no longer in its infancy. Increasing responsibility and accountability are entirely appropriate.

Words, pictures and videos on the internet can be useful tools. There can be circumstances where it is entirely appropriate to prevent those tools from being weaponized. Courts have been treating Section 230 as a Super-First Amendment, even though courts have long recognized the many exceptions to the language of the First Amendment. "[O]f the twenty-five most popular U.S. websites, eighteen allowed public user content. All those sites had adopted user content policies that addressed, at minimum, illegal activities, hate speech, harassment, bullying, distribution of personal information, nudity or pornography, and violent content."[157]

It is difficult to maintain public faith in online platforms unless they do a better job at moderation.

Even when confronted with heartbreaking tragedies where an internet platform (backpage.com) aided and abetted rapes and murders of children, courts have clung to the view that if the evils of the modern internet are deemed to outweigh the First Amendment values that drive the CDA, the remedy is through legislation, not through litigation.[158]

There are other reasons to allow civil litigation against providers or users of an interactive computer service. Juries ought to be able to tell whether fault should be assigned where it is due, and the extent of the damages due and owing. Further, the standard of proof in civil litigation is the relatively easy one of "preponderance of the evidence". Criminal prosecution requires proof beyond a reasonable doubt. It is therefore possible for civil litigation to right more wrongs and clean up more bad situations.

Our system must have strong criminal penalties and civil remedies for cyber-harassment, online bullying, and life-changing defamation. Babies need special protections like cribs and playpens. Infant internet industries needed the protection of Section 230. In the year 2020, the internet is (or should have) grown up. Section 230 is a relic of a simpler time in Internet history. It is time to require the internet industry to be more responsible and accountable.

We modern people do tend to be fond of our technology. Recall the panic when the Blackberry servers went down for a few hours.

All the Crackberry addicts were sweating profusely. Norms are essential for a civilized society. The internet provided the opportunity to experiment to a certain extent with variations in norms. As with many experiments, some changes were failures. The successes have been awesome. Norms can sometimes change according to societal feedback. Where the internet has infantile areas or adolescent areas, adult supervision can be an improvement.[159]

Congress is good at aiming for a middle-of-the-road compromise. There may have been a somewhat less than perfect communication between the legislative and judicial branches. The rapidly changing circumstances of the internet have progressed to the point where it is necessary for Congress and the courts to re-adjust the law.

But even with that recognition, the broad construction of CDA's immunity provision adopted by the courts has produced an immunity from liability far more sweeping than anything the law's words, context, and history support. Platforms have been protected from liability even though they republished content knowing it might violate the law; encouraged users to post illegal content; changed their design and policies to enable illegal activity; or sold dangerous products. As a result, hundreds of decisions have extended §230 immunity, with comparatively few denying or restricting it.

Whether wrongdoing on the internet requires criminal prosecution and punishment or a civil suit and payment, there shouldn't be much difference between internet law and real-life law. Absent a Supreme Court intervention, the ship may have sailed in regards to the judiciary's interpretation of the current statute.

§230 immunity has been invoked by giant companies engaged in enterprises that have little to do with free expression. This is true for Airbnb, which facilitates short-term rentals of real estate and eBay, which runs an auction site. It is not hard to see §230's immunity being asserted by Uber, which arranges transportation. Other online applications might assert §230 immunity, such as an on-demand massage service; or a company which sends hair stylists to people's homes. These businesses have little to do with free expression, though we have seen business in the on-demand economy asserting section 230's protection, with some success. If those companies operated in brick and mortar places, they could not escape liability for failing to meet reasonable duties of care.

Landlords, shopping malls, hospitals, and banks have been held liable for enabling foreseeable criminal activity of third parties, but the "The judiciary needs to be bolder in carving out tort duties to compensate the victims of cyber-wrongs...."[160] Tobacco litigation and the prospect of handgun litigation may have an influence on the future of internet tort litigation.[161] Even though tort law should provide remedies for (1) public disclosure of private facts, (2) intrusion on seclusion, (3) depiction of another in a false light, and (4) appropriation of another's image for commercial gain, the reality of how courts work is ill-suited to provide actual remedies.[162] Due to the extraordinary power of the modern internet, it may be that wrongs that did not warrant judicial remedies in the past should in the present and even more so should in the future.[163] Congress did not even prohibit holding providers liable for the dissemination of information; it merely prohibited a finding that a provider was a "publisher" or "speaker." Liability for aiding and abetting others' wrongful acts does not depend on the manner in which aid was provided. Designing a site to enable defamation or sex trafficking could result in liability in the absence of a finding that a site was being sued for publishing or speaking.

Congress should establish a reasonable standard of care that will reduce opportunities for abuses without interfering with further development of a vibrant internet. Reaching such an honorable comprise requires moving beyond how the hyper-protective stage has currently mired many courts.

The National Institute of Justice explains that the ubiquity of the Internet and the ease with which it allows others unusual access to personal information make individuals more accessible and vulnerable to online abuse. Harassing people online is far cheaper and less personally risky than confronting them in real space.[164]

If victims seek legal help, they are accused of endangering the Internet as a forum of public discourse. Defendants proclaim the Internet is a free speech zone, a virtual Wild West, that cannot and should not bear the weight of regulation, commenters say. Victims are told not to expect any help. Defendants say "This is the INTERNET folks…. There are no laws here, at least not clearly defined ones."[165]

Normally, the law can subject publishers to tort liability for defamations they publish.[166] The law can also subject publishers to liability for publications that created an unreasonable risk of the solicitation and commission of violent criminal activity.[167] Not long ago, the law didn't provide any remedy for workplace sexual harassment or domestic violence. Now it does. Change is possible.

True legal innovation also means moving beyond a focus on harassers as the sole problem and addressing the responsibilities of a narrow class of online service providers: sites that encourage cyber stalking or nonconsensual pornography and make money from its removal or that principally host cyber stalking or nonconsensual pornography.[168] We need to enhance criminal, tort, and civil rights laws' ability to deter and punish wrongdoers.

§230(c) is part of what has surely become one of the most striking misnomers on the books: the Communications Decency Act of 1996. Two entirely different brands of discourse have developed. In the traditional media, things remain reasonably decorous. But online the promise of anonymity, though far flimsier than most suspect, unlocks something ugly and menacing in ostensibly normal people. And while anything goes in the Google era, everything also stays, and spreads. The whole world is now the bathroom wall, and that wall can never be entirely painted over.

There may need to be a sea change in American tort law regarding defamation on the internet. In the American Old Wild West, if somebody got defamed, her or she could pack up and move someplace else. Nowadays, the internet is everywhere.

The controversy about applicability of the immunity of § 230 to State criminal laws is interesting.[169] The nature of the internet and internet crimes tends to indicate Federal law is often the proper perspective and basis for prosecution of internet crimes, but if a State has statutes describing crimes and internet companies committed the crimes (or aided and abetted the crimes or conspired to commit the crimes), then logic would indicate it would be proper for State authorities to prosecute the crimes.

For example, Washington State makes it a crime to post intimate pictures without consent. If Washington State prosecutors decided to charge TheDirty.com with conspiracy to commit the crime and being an accomplice in committing the crime, the website would try to raise a defense based on § 230. Such a defense should fail, but how an individual judge would rule is somewhat unpredictable.

Privacy torts may have the potential to chill speech, but they also serve to protect people's ability to engage in expressive activities free from fear of social disapproval.[170]

The development of new electronic media for social communication has made broadcasting of one's views possible for an unprecedented number of people. The injury and scorn that such a broadcast may subject the person who is defamed is therefore much more serious and widespread when using electronic media. In contrast to print, electronic media are extremely fast in their dissemination of views, to the point of going "viral" or duplicating themselves millions of times in a few minutes. Courts have made reference to the fact that many newer forms of publication are not readily analyzed by the traditional definitions of libel and slander, simply because advanced technology has made these definitions obsolete. However, this does not mean that these newer technologies will help wrongdoers to escape the consequences of defaming others, whether by print, oral or electronic media. Conversely, users of the internet need to exercise extreme caution in the statements they make lest they become subjects of defamation suits with the potential of high damages.[171]

To date most cyber torts remain elusive from legal sanctions for a number of reasons.[172] In a situation where there is no literal damage to physical property nor is there physical bodily harm, courts and juries might not want to worry about it. Cyber-Tort law is still in a fledgling stage of development. It is quite a challenge for anybody to obtain any form of judgment against another for a Cyber-Tort. Persons who have been victims of a Cyber-Tort face an uphill battle if they choose to seek redress in the form of a civil suit.

Company policies can help. Part of Facebook's policy says "Facebook does not tolerate bullying or harassment. We allow users to speak freely on matters and people of public interest, but take action on all reports of abusive behavior directed at private individuals."

Facebook explains to users that cyber bullying and harassment involve the repeated targeting of private individuals, inflicting emotional distress. YouTube's community guidelines say "We want you to use YouTube without fear of being subjected to malicious harassment. In cases where harassment crosses the line into a malicious attack it can be reported and will be removed. In other cases, users may be mildly annoying or petty and should simply be ignored."

Section 230 tries to define "provider of interactive computer service" by specifically mentioning libraries and educational institutions. Okay, fine, it is rare for anybody to want to see libraries and educational institutions getting sued. But Congress may not have been envisioning TheDirty.com or RipoffReport.com. In fact, the very title of the Communication Decency Act indicates Congress was trying to increase decency in communications, not immunize the indecent. Popular websites do tend to have internal policies and terms of use that they design with profitability and popularity in mind. Conscientious moderation promotes civility and prohibits crime.

Nobody really believes the world is better without privacy. Social media can have a tremendous impact on politics. Some people believe the most desirable option for moderating content is to apply pressure on internet companies to promote, implement, and approve a self-regulatory model with transparency and accountability.

The controversy between the desire to protect vulnerable populations versus the inclination to allow the market to naturally regulate itself continues.[173] The internet may eventually transcend borders and territorial rule. Presently, though, governments continue to exert their influence to control the web (*i.e.* Google's struggle to do business in France and Yahoo's compliance with Chinese censorship).[174]

Internet Service Providers have an almost insurmountable incumbent's advantage, like AT&T did with the wired phone network back in the twentieth century.[175]

The Internet occupies a fascinating position in modern society. Some have compared its function to the way town squares have functioned for as long as there have been town squares. Both can be a place for people to make friends, catch the latest news, form communities, or buy and sell goods and services. The differences are unlike anything we've seen before: a supra-national world, often with near complete anonymity, and an ability to reach to all corners of the earth. People have been concerned by the ability to regulate access and activity on the internet since the very first years of its creation. Recently this has resurfaced with the discussion on Net

Neutrality in the United States, and the Right to Be Forgotten in Europe and Argentina.

So, should Governments step into cyberspace to exert their influences? Can they? Does an unregulated internet represent societies' best hope for freedom and liberty, or is it merely an excuse for criminal elements, corporate forces, and renegade wrongdoers to evade crucial checks and balances?[176]

The growing debate continues regarding whether existing controls on Internet content adequately meet the concerns of users and what happens when the heavily regulated world of broadcasting collides with the virtually unregulated world of the Internet.[177]

The example of the events of the "Arab Spring" show the power and potential power of the internet.[178],[179]

Aside from blatant censorship of the Internet in nations like China, Saudi Arabia, or Iran, it has been postulated that there are four primary modes of regulation of the internet: Laws, Architecture, Norms, and Markets.[180]

1. Laws may be the most obvious form of regulation. Various states, countries, and international groups are attempting to grapple with issues raised by the use of the Internet. They normally effect their policies through the implementation of laws. Such regulations can include statutory laws and common law. Laws may have the shortcoming of limited

geographical scope. Compliance with varying and sometimes conflicting laws might be difficult or impossible or undesirable.

2. Architecture can limit the internet. Where information can or cannot be transmitted across the Internet because of physical limitations. "Architecture" can refer to everything from internet filtering software, to firewalls, to encryption programs, and even the basic structure of internet transmission protocols, like TCP/IP. In many ways, it is the most fundamental form of Internet regulation, and all other areas of Cyberlaw must relate to or rely upon it in some fashion since it is, quite literally, how the Internet is made.

3. Norms are very important online or offline. They refer to the ways in which people interact with one another. As social norms govern what is or is not appropriate in regular society, norms affect behavior across the Internet. While laws can fail to regulate certain activities allowed by the architecture of the internet, social norms can allow the users to control such conduct. Many online forums allow users to moderate comments made by other users. Comments found to be offensive or off topic can be flagged and removed. Such capabilities are a form of norm regulation.

4. Market regulation is similar to norm regulation. Market regulation can control patterns of conduct on the internet by the

traditional economic principles of supply and demand. Something unpopular will lack a demand. It will eventually fail. If there is excessive supply, competitors will eventually have to find ways to differentiate themselves or become obscured by the competition. Market regulation helps to prevent predatory conduct, drive innovation, and forces websites to self-regulate in order to retain customers and remain viable.

America is the land of the free and the home of the brave. We treasure the heritage of the Wild West and have glorified Cyberspace as the new Wild West, but we have glossed over the unacceptable brutal problems of the Wild West and Cyberspace.

"Other jurisdictions—even Western democracies such as Europe and Canada—provide weaker protections for distributors of third-party content. Typically, if a website receives a complaint about an allegedly defamatory or illegal user post, it must remove the content immediately or be forced to defend its legality in court."[181]

§230 is increasingly under attack as trolls and criminals figure out new ways to exploit the Internet. According to many critics, §230 enables terrorist recruitment, discriminatory housing sales, online sex trafficking, and vicious harassment.

Issues about the World Wide Web require consideration of the world wide situation. If the USA had stricter regulations about online third-party speech, ISPs might relocate to countries that had more relaxed standards.

Section 230's protections for online platforms are not a constitutional mandate, but a policy choice of Congress. Historically, bookstores and newsstands have some protection regarding materials created by others, especially if the intermediaries didn't know the materials were illegal. Courts have wanted to avoid a chilling effect on free speech. It's hard not to agree with a "don't shoot the messenger" doctrine, but if the messenger is also a sender of a message, then it is a different situation. Likewise, if a messenger knows he is carrying a bomb, then he should be held responsible.

People like to be able to send as well as receive, but nobody likes to be the object of false, defamatory lies.

There is a difference between a publisher and a bookstore (or newsstand or library). "Publish" means "To make public; to circulate; to make known to people in general ...."[182] The debate shifted from a focus on state of mind to one of editorial control.

Significant factors can include (1) editorial control, and (2) knowledge of objectionable content.

Cyber-Torts
Page 136

There were true benefits of emerging communication technologies, but problems arose about racism, obscenity, criminal fraud, and wrongful defamatory lies. Words can help or hurt. Words can stop things from happening or make things happen. ISPs have a decision to make about what extent they will reserve the right to remove objectionable content. The law tends not to want to change. Significant changes in technology can require re-thinking some established legal principles.

The tech industry's sustainability and growth are important, but individual rights are also crucial.

In general, accountability and responsibility are necessary for any civilized society. Those who make fraudulent, criminal or false defamatory lies on the internet should be held responsible and accountable. In order for that to happen, it would be necessary to require identification of internet users. We require identification of automobile drivers because automobiles are powerful instrumentalities. Computers on the internet are also powerful instrumentalities. Karl Benz patented what is generally considered the first modern car in 1886.[183] American States started issuing driver's licenses in 1903. By 1954, all States required driver's licenses. The FCC requires licensing for radio and television broadcasting. It might not be unreasonable to require some kind of identification of internet users.

Wide immunity to internet companies for scurrilous user posts might not be popular currently.

The drafters of §230 wanted to avoid freezing innovation and they succeeded. Unfortunately, boiling can be as dangerous as freezing. A middle ground compromise is often the proper goal.

In the years following the enactment of §230, contemporaneous decisions were vigorously disputed,[184] but the tide of judicial opinion was flowing towards interpreting §230 as bulletproof.

Amazement at the wonder and beauty of the internet and the dazzling quantities of money internet companies have been gathering appears to have clouded judicial opinions in interpreting §230 as being more airtight that it should be.[185]

There should not be broad automatic immunity of the most callous and damaging defamation that anyone might maliciously post on the Internet.[186]

In addition to defamation, causes of action may also include invasion of privacy, negligence, and misappropriation of right of publicity.[187]

The early judicial interpretation of Section 230 encouraged the creation and growth of

American internet companies. Excluding China (which closes off much of its Internet access to outside companies), thirteen of the largest sixteen Internet companies are based in the United States.

By 2009, the Internet was no longer a nascent technology. User content–focused platforms such as Facebook and Yelp had evolved from start-ups into large businesses. More and more people—including judges—were starting to question why Section 230 afforded extraordinary benefits to the specific category of thriving business.

In adjusting the law, it is important to avoid letting the pendulum swing too far in the other direction. The law should be in the middle between the competing interests of individual liberty versus the common good.

Conclusion

In the age of newspapers, it was traditional wisdom to avoid picking a fight with somebody who buys his ink by the barrel. Nowadays, everybody with internet access has a figurative barrel of ink. Nonetheless, ownership of a barrel of ink should not give anybody immunity from liability for splashing it around wildly. We can be certain that cyber torts will continue to occur, as surely as we can foresee that there will be circumstances where reasonable minds can differ. Striking a balance between the interests of competing parties is the goal. In a world where the rights and freedoms of individuals and groups will inevitably compete with each other, the capacity to resolve conflicts through civil discourse and civil litigation is an essential feature for the maintenance and improvement of life and liberty. Making the world a better place is an enormous job. The sooner we get started, the better.

There should be more jury trials about internet cases. Juries don't necessarily fall into the traps that Congress and judges do, placing an undue emphasis on profits, power, and prestige. Juries can bring reason and logic to proceedings if allowed to do so. It can be about the truth and the justice.

Where users commit torts, other users should have a right to respond and seek remedies. Providers should have to make it easy for victims to give notice of wrongdoing. Providers should create and implement policies that require reporting to government about crime. Providers should encourage and facilitate due process of law in civil matters.

The internet empowers people. Government should discourage the empowerment of character assassins and mischief makers.

Questions for Discussion

1. Who is in a position to regulate the internet?
2. Who is competent to regulate the internet?
3. Would we trust internet geeks to judge whether content is objectionable?
4. Would we trust government wonks to judge whether content is objectionable?
5. What would be the effect of categorizing platform owners as "distributors" rather than "publishers"?
6. Should the law of the internet be the same as the law of a particular political jurisdiction – or – a world-wide law – or – some other formulation of morality and reality?
7. What if a website promotes terrorism?
8. So, if the internet is like the Wild West, where is the Lone Ranger? Where is Matt Dillon?
9. What if Congress meant well, but failed to foresee the consequences in later years of their vagueness regarding the distinction between "publisher" and "distributor"?
10. Should ISPs be exposed to multimillion-dollar lawsuits because they try to moderate third-party content?
11. What about identification for internet users?

Notes

[1] Nonnenmacher, Tomas. "History of the U.S. Telegraph Industry". EH.Net Encyclopedia, edited by Robert Whaples. August 14, 2001. URL http://eh.net/encyclopedia/history-of-the-u-s-telegraph-industry/

[2] Morrison, Sharon L.. "Radio Act of 1912". https://mtsu.edu/first-amendment/article/1090/radio-act-of-1912

[3] Skretvedt, Randy and Sterling, Christopher H. "Radio." https://www.britannica.com/topic/radio; https://www.fcc.gov/document/radio-act-1927-established-federal-radio-commission;

[4] https://transition.fcc.gov/Reports/1934new.pdf

[5] https://www.fcc.gov/media/television/television

[6] Kosseff, Jeff. The Twenty-Six Words That Created the Internet. Cornell U. Press (Ithaca & London, 2019).

[7] *Reno v. American Civil Liberties Union*, 521 U.S. 844 (1997)

[8] *United States v. Morris*, 928 F.2d 504 (2d Cir. 1991).

[9] *United States v. Riggs*, 739 F.Supp. 414, 743 F.Supp. 556 (1990); 967 F.2d 561 (11th Cir. 1990)

[10] https://www.deepdyve.com/lp/elsevier/in-rindos-v-hardwick-dafkkalZlC

11
http://dictionary.sensagent.com/rindos%20v%20hardwick/
en-en/

12 https://www.statista.com/statistics/273018/number-of-
internet-users-
worldwide/#:~:text=In%202019%2C%20the%20number%
20of%20internet%20users%20worldwide,the%20internet
%20more%20frequently%20and%20with%20more%20co
nvenience.

13 Davidson, Jacob. "Here's How Many Internet Users
There Are (in 2020)". Money.com. (May 19, 2020 1:48 PM
ET.)

14 https://merchdope.com/youtube-stats/

15 https://www.internetlivestats.com/twitter-statistics/

16
https://web.archive.org/web/20190722203322/https://www
.cision.com/us/2019/01/top-ten-us-daily-newspapers/

17 https://www.oberlo.com/blog/twitter-statistics

18 *Ibid.*

19 https://www.bloomberg.com/quote/TWTR:US

20 *Osmond v. EWAP*, 153 Cal.App.3d 842, 847 (Cal. Ct.
App. 1984).

21 Kosseff, Jeff. The Twenty-Six Words That Created the
Internet . Cornell University Press. Kindle Edition.

22 Ammori, Marvin. "The New York Times: Free Speech

Cyber-Torts

Lawyering in the Age of Google and Twitter." 127 Harv. L. Rev. 2259, 2260 (2014); Jack M. Balkin, The Future of Free Expression in a Digital Age, 36 Pepp. L. Rev. 427 (2009).

[23] *Fair Housing Council v. Roommates.com*, 521 F.3d 1157 (9th Cir. 2008) (*en banc*).

[24] *Farmers Educational & Cooperative Union of America, North Dakota Division v. WDAY, Inc.*, 360 U.S. 525 (1959),

[25] *Smith v. California*, 361 US 147 (1959).

[26] *Farmers Educational & Cooperative Union of America, North Dakota Division v. WDAY, Inc.*, 360 U.S. 525, 529–530 (1959).

[27] *Smith v. California*, 361 US 147, 172 n.1 (1959); Kosseff, Jeff. The Twenty-Six Words That Created the Internet . Cornell University Press. Kindle Edition.

[28] *Cubby v. CompuServe*, 776 F.Supp. 135 (S.D.N.Y. 1991).

[29] *Cubby v. CompuServe,* 90 Civ. 6571 (S.D.N.Y. Oct. 5, 1990).

[30] *Stratton Oakmont v. Prodigy Services Co.*, Index No. 94–031063 (N.Y. Sup. Ct., Nassau County, Jan. 9, 1995). https://h2o.law.harvard.edu/cases/4540

[31] https://www.fcc.gov/general/telecommunications-act-1996

[32] *Quoted* in In *Barrett v. Rosenthal*, 146 P.3d 510 (CA

Supreme Ct. 2006), where the court admitted that "recognizing broad immunity for defamatory republications on the Internet has some troubling consequences."

[33] *Reno v. American Civil Liberties Union*, 521 U.S. 844 (1997).

[34] *Reno v. American Civil Liberties Union, supra*, 521 U.S. at p. 880.

[35] *Zeran v. America Online*, 129 F.3d 327 (4th Cir. 1997) cert. denied, 524 U.S. 937, 118 S. Ct. 2341, 141 L. Ed. 2d 712 (1998)

[36] *Zeran v. America Online, Inc.*, 129 F.3d 327, 330 (4th Cir. 1997), https://law.justia.com/cases/federal/appellate-courts/F3/129/327/621462/

[37] Goldman, Eric. "The Ten Most Important Section 230 Rulings." Tul. J. Tech. & Intell. Prop. 1 (2017).

[38] *citing* W. Page Keeton et al., Prosser and Keeton on the Law of Torts § 113, at 810 (5th ed.1984).

[39] *Stratton Oakmont, Inc. v. Prodigy Servs. Co.*, 1995 WL 323710 (N.Y.Sup.Ct. May 24, 1995)

[40] *Zeran v. Diamond Broadcasting*, 203 F.3d 714 (10th Cir. 2000).

[41] *Barrett v. Rosenthal*, 146 P.3d 510 (CA Supreme Ct. 2006).

[42] *Blumenthal v. Drudge and AOL*, 992 F. Supp. 44, 51–52 (D.D.C. 1998).

[43] http://www.dmlp.org/threats/blumenthal-v-drudge

[44] *Doe v. America Online*, 783 So.2d 1010 (Fl. 2001).

[45] Davidson, Stephen J. *et al.* "The Law of Cyberspace Liability of Information Service Providers." 574 Prac. L. Inst. 143, 155 (2000)

[46] *Schneider v. Amazon.com, Inc.*, 108 Wn. App. 454, 31 P.3d 37 (2001).

[47] *Batzel v. Smith*, 333 F.3d 1018 (9th Cir. 2003).

[48] *See also Batzel v. Smith*, 351 F. 3d 904 (2003) (Gould, J., dissenting from denial of rehearing en banc) and *Batzel v. Smith*, 372 F. Supp.2d 546 (C.D. Cal. 2005).

[49] *Batzel v. Smith*, 333 F.3d 1018 ((9th Cir. 2003).

[50] *Carafano v. Metrosplash*, 339 F.3d 119 (9th Cir. 2003).

[51] *Carafano v. Metrosplash*, 207 F. Supp. 2d 1055 (C.D. Cal. 2002).

[52] https://en.wikipedia.org/wiki/John_Seigenthaler

[53] *Barrett v. Rosenthal*, 146 P.3d 510 (CA Supreme Ct. 2006)

[54] Jenal, James. "When Is a User Not a "User"? Finding the Proper Role for Republication Liability on the Internet" 24 Loy.L.A. Ent. L.Rev. 453 (2004)

[55] (*Id.* at pp. 477-480.)

[56] *Quoting Donato v. Moldow*, 865 A.2d 711, 725 (N.J.

Super. Ct. 2005).

57 Chander, Anupam. "How Law Made Silicon Valley." 63 Emory L.J. 639, 650 (2014)(providing a thorough catalog of cases interpreting Section 230).

58 *Global Royalties, Ltd. v Xcentric Ventures, LLC*, 544 F. Supp. 2d 929 (D. Ariz., 2008)

59 Sieminski, Paul & Hogan, Holly. "The Automatic Doctrine: Why (Allegedly) Defamatory Content on WordPress.com Doesn't Come Down without a Court Order". TechDirt (Feb. 7, 2018).

60 *Zango, Inc. v. Kaspersky Lab, Inc.*, 568 F.3d 1169 (9th Cir. 2009).

61 Goldman, Eric. "The Ten Most Important Section 230 Rulings." Tul. J. Tech. & Intell. Prop. 1 (2017).

62 *Blockowicz v. Williams*, 630 F.3d 563 (7th Cir. 2010).

63 *Doe v. MySpace*, 528 F. 3d 413 (5th Cir. 2008).

64 Zetter, Kim. "Judge Acquits Lori Drew in Cyberbullying Case, Overrules Jury" (2009) available at https://www.wired.com/2009/07/drew_court/

65 *Jones v. Dirty World Entertainment Recordings LLC*, 755 F. 3d 398 (6th Cir. 2014).

66 Kosseff, Jeff. The Twenty-Six Words That Created the Internet . Cornell University Press. Kindle Edition.

67 https://thedirty.com/legal-faqs/

[68] *See also*: *Jones v. Dirty World Entertainment Recordings*, 840 F. Supp. 2d 1008, 1009 (E.D. Ky. 2012).

[69] Teachers Can't Be Cheerleaders, The Dirty, available at https://gossip.thedirty.com/gossip/cincinnati/teachers-cant-be-cheerleaders/#post-241723.

[70] Bengals Cheerleader Gets Engaged to the Teen She Was Convicted of Having Underage Sex With, Daily Mail (June 13, 2013).

[71] Citron, Danielle Keats & Wittes, Benjamin. "The Internet Will Not Break: Denying Bad Samaritans Section 230 Immunity." 86 Fordham L. Rev. 401 (2018).

[72] Part of the reasoning of *New York Times v. Sullivan*, 376 US 254 (1964) and *Gertz v. Welch*, 418 US 323, 344 (1974) was that public figures had access to the media to respond and rebut wrongful speech, but now it is common for people to have access to the capability to respond over the internet. Perhaps courts should re-evaluate the public figure / private individual distinction in light of the facts.

[73] *Kimzey v. Yelp! Inc.*, 836 F. 3d 1263 (9th Cir. 2016).

[74] *New York Times Co. v. Sullivan*, 376 U.S. 254 (1964)

[75] *Gertz v. Robert Welch, Inc.*, 418 U.S. 323 (1974).

[76] *Erie Railroad Co. v. Tompkins*, 304 U.S. 64 (1938).

[77] Kosseff, Jeff. The Twenty-Six Words That Created the Internet . Cornell University Press. Kindle Edition.

[78] Barbour, Emily. "The SPEECH Act: the Federal Response to 'Libel Tourism'". Congressional Research Service, 2010).

[79] Rosen, Jeffrey. "The Right to Be Forgotten." Stan. L. Rev. (Feb. 2012).

[80] Schroeder, Stan. "Google Has Received Nearly 350,000 URL Removal Requests So Far." Mashable (Nov. 26, 2015).

[81] Kosseff, Jeffrey. "How do you change the most important law in Internet history? Carefully." ARStechnica (12/23/2017, 6:36 AM).

[82] Kosseff, Jeff. The Twenty-Six Words That Created the Internet. Cornell University Press. Kindle Edition.

[83] *Ibid*.

[84] Kosseff, Jeff. The Twenty-Six Words That Created the Internet. Cornell University Press. Kindle Edition.

[85] *Barnes v. Yahoo!, Inc.*, 570 F. 3d 1096, 1107 (9th Cir. 2009). https://www.eff.org/files/barnes-v-yahoo.pdf

[86] *Doe v. Internet Brands*, 767 F. 3d 894, 898 (9th Cir. 2014). https://cite.case.law/f3d/767/894/

[87] Fair Housing Council of San Fernando Valley v. Roommates.com, 521 F.3d 1157, (9th Cir. 2008) (en banc).

[88] *Fair Housing Council v. Roommate.com*, 666 F.3d 1215 (9th Cir. 2012).

[89] *Fair Housing Council of San Fernando Valley v. Roommates.com*, 521 F.3d 1157 (9th Cir. 2008) (*en banc*).

[90] *Fair Housing Council v. Roommate.com*, 666 F.3d 1215 (9th Cir. 2012).

[91] *FTC v. Accusearch*, 570 F.3d 1187 (10th Cir. 2009).

[92] *Barnes v. Yahoo!, Inc.*, 570 F. 3d 1096 (9th Cir. 2009).

[93] https://h2o.law.harvard.edu/cases/101

[94] *See also Barnes v. Yahoo*, Civil Action No. 6:05-CV-926-AA (D. Or. June 23, 2005)

[95] *Doe v. Internet Brands*, 824 F.3d 846 (9th Cir. 2016).

[96] See also *Doe v. Internet Brands*, 767 F. 3d 894 (9th Cir. 2014).

[97] *Doe v. Internet Brands*, Case 2:12-cv-03626-JFW-PJW (C.D. Cal. April 26, 2012); *Waitt v. Internet Brands*, 2:10-cv-03006-GHK-JCG (C.D. Cal. Sept. 22, 2010); *Doe v. Internet Brands*, Case No. 12–56638 (9th Cir. March 15, 2013).

[98] *But see* "Doe v. Internet Brands, Inc. - Ninth Circuit Declines to Extend § 230 Immunity to Failure-to-Warn Claims". 130 Harv. L. Rev. 777 (Dec. 9, 2016)

[99] *Diamond Ranch Academy v. Filer*, No. 2:2014cv00751 - Document 55 (D. Utah 2015)

[100] Kosseff, Jeff. "Twenty Years of Intermediary Immunity: The US Experience", (2017) 14:1 SCRIPTed 5

Cyber-Torts

https://script-ed.org/?p=3309. DOI:
10.2966/scrip.140117.5

101 Citron, Danielle Keats & Wittes, Benjamin. "The
Internet Will Not Break: Denying Bad Samaritans Section
230 Immunity." 86 Fordham L. Rev 401 (2017).

102 *J.S. v. Vill. Voice Media Holdings, LLC*, 184 Wn.2d 95,
359 P.3d 714 (2015),

103 https://www.youtube.com/watch?v=D24zYQcnqKs

104 Shinder, Deb. "What makes cybercrime laws so
difficult to enforce." Techrepublic, January 26, 2011, 4:05
AM PST.

105 *In re Anonymous Online Speakers*, 661 F.3d 1168 (9th
Cir. 2011).

106 https://www.cbsnews.com/news/obama-eyeing-
internet-id-for-americans/

107 Pearlman, Jeff. "Tracking Down My Online Haters,"
CNN, January 21, 2011, http://articles.cnn.com/2011-01-
21/opinion/pearlman.online.civility_1_online-haters-twitter-
online-behavior?_s=PM:OPINION.

108 Dawson, Joe. "Who Is That? The Study of Anonymity
and Behavior." Psychological Science. (March 30, 2018).
https://www.psychologicalscience.org/observer/who-is-
that-the-study-of-anonymity-and-behavior

109 *Fields v. Twitter*, Case No. 3:16-cv-213-WHO (N.D.
Cal. Mar. 24, 2016).

110 Citron, Danielle Keats. Hate Crimes in Cyberspace.

Harvard University Press. Kindle Edition.

[111] https://www.theguardian.com/uk-news/2013/sep/03/caroline-criado-perez-rape-threats-continue

[112] See Citron, Danielle Keats. "Extremist Speech, Compelled Conformity, and Censorship Creep". 93 Notre Dame L. Rev. 1035 (2018).

[113] Clarke, Richard A. and Knake, Robert K. Cyber War – The Next Threat to National Security and What to Do About It. (Harper-Collins, 2010).

[114] *See, e.g.* RCW 5.40.050 (https://app.leg.wa.gov/RCW/default.aspx?cite=5.40.050).

[115] *Varian Med. Sys. v. Delfino*, 113 Cal.App.4th 273 (Cal. Ct. App. 2003).

[116] Circuit Court for the 17th Judicial Circuit, Broward County, Florida, Case Number: CACE03022837

[117] https://usatoday30.usatoday.com/news/nation/2006-10-10-internet-defamation-case_x.htm

[118] http://www.dmlp.org/threats/scheff-v-bock

[119] Sydell, Laura. "Calif. Bans Jilted Lovers from Posting 'Revenge Porn' Online." NPR October 2, 2013).

[120] Morrison, Patt. "Column: Holly Jacobs on making 'revenge porn' a federal crime in the wake of the Katie Hill fiasco." LA Times (Nov. 6, 2019, 2 AM)

[121] https://www.latimes.com/opinion/story/2019-11-06/holly-jacobs-revenge-porn-katie-hill-federal-law

[122] RCW 9A.86
(https://app.leg.wa.gov/RCW/default.aspx?cite=9A.86)

[123] *Doe v. Backpage*, 817 F.3d 12 (1st Cir. 2016).

[124] https://www.leagle.com/decision/infco20160314075

[125] Strochlic, Nina. "Uber: Disabilities Laws Don't Apply to Us." The Daily Beast (May 21, 2015).

[126] Wieczner, Jen. "Why the Disabled Are Suing Uber and Lyft". TIME (May 22, 2015), http://time.com/3895021/whythe-disabled-are-suing-uber-and-lyft/.

[127] Munson, Lee. "Revenge Porn Operator Faces Charges on Conspiracy, Extortion, and Identity Theft," Naked Security, December 11, 2013, http://nakedsecurity.sophos.com/2013/12/11/revenge-porn-operator-facing-charges-of-conspiracy-extortion-and-identity-theft/.

[128] https://www.cbsnews.com/news/man-charged-in-running-revenge-porn-site-convicted/

[129] Zabala, Liberty and Stickney, R. ""Revenge Porn" Defendant Sentenced to 18 Years." NBCSanDiego (April 3, 6, 2015.) https://www.nbcsandiego.com/news/local/kevin-bollaert-revenge-porn-sentencing-san-diego/1992395/

[130] Wagner, David. "How to Prosecute a Revenge Porn Profiteer," National Public Radio (KPBS San Francisco),

December 17, 2013,
http://www.kpbs.org/news/2013/dec/17/how-prosecute-revenge-porn-profiteer/.

131 https://merchdope.com/youtube-stats/

132 Karst, Kenneth L. "Threats and Meanings: How the Facts Govern First Amendment Doctrine," Stanford Law Review 58 (2006): 1337–1412, 1345.

133 Citron, Danielle Keats. Hate Crimes in Cyberspace (p. 228). Harvard University Press. Kindle Edition. (Quoted.)

134 Bartow, Ann. "Online Harassment, Profit Seeking, and Section 230." B.U. L. Rev. Online (Nov. 2, 2015).

135 *Knight First Amendment Inst. At Columbia Univ. v. Trump*, 302 F. Supp. 3d 541, 579 (S.D.N.Y. 2018); *Knight First Amendment Institute et al. v. Trump*, No. 18-1691 (2nd Cir. 2019) (https://law.justia.com/cases/federal/appellate-courts/ca2/18-1691/18-1691-2019-07-09.html)

136 *Obsidian Finance v. Cox*, case No. 12-35238 (9th Cir., 2014). http://cdn.ca9.uscourts.gov/datastore/opinions/2014/01/17/12-35238.pdf

137 *Southeastern Promotions, Ltd. v. Conrad*, 420 U.S. 546 (1975).

138 Harvard Law Review. "Recent Case: Knight First Amendment Institute at Columbia University v. Trump". June 3, 2019. https://blog.harvardlawreview.org/recent-case-knight-first-amendment-institute-at-columbia-university-v-trump/]

Cyber-Torts

[139] Carey, Nick. "In Libya, the cellphone as weapon." Technology News, August 23, 2011. https://www.reuters.com/article/us-libya-misrata-idUSTRE77M38520110823

[140] *Knight* at 29 (2nd Cir., 2019.

[141] *Davison v. Randall*, 912 F.3d 666 (4th Cir. 2019) https://www.leagle.com/decision/infco20190107043

[142] *N.Y. Times Co. v. Sullivan*, 376 U.S. 254 (1964).

[143] See *Blumenthal v. Drudge*, 992 F. Supp. 44, 49 (D.D.C. 1998).

[144] *Virginia v. Black*, 538 U.S. 343, 359 (2003).

[145] Citron, Danielle Keats. Hate Crimes in Cyberspace (p. 217). Harvard University Press. Kindle Edition.

[146] *Chicago Lawyers' Committee for Civil Rights Under Law, Inc. v. Craigslist, Inc.*, 519 F.3d 666 (7th Cir. 2008)

[147] https://www.law.cornell.edu/uscode/text/47/230

[148] Allyn, Bobby. "Stung by Twitter, Trump Signs Executive Order to Weaken Social Media Companies". NPR, May 28, 2020, 4:59 PM ET. https://www.npr.org/2020/05/28/863932758/stung-by-twitter-trump-signs-executive-order-to-weaken-social-media-companies

[149] Faulders, Katherine and Cathey, Libby. "Trump signs executive order targeting social media companies...." ABCnews. (May 28, 2020, 4:06 PM).

Cyber-Torts
Page 156

https://abcnews.go.com/Politics/trump-sign-executive-order-targeting-social-media-companies/story?id=70925213

[150] Tribe, Laurence H. and Geltzer, Joshua A. "Trump is doubly wrong about Twitter." Washington Post May 28, 2020. https://www.washingtonpost.com/

Bell, Karissa. "Mark Zuckerberg and Jack Dorsey disagree on fact checking the president." Engadget, May 28, 2020. https://www.engadget.com/mark-zuckerberg-jack-dorsey-trump-fact-check-203836979.html

[151] Nelson, Steven. "Trump writes 'Revoke 230!' after Twitter masks George Floyd tweets." NY Post. (May 29, 2020 | 12:34pm); https://nypost.com/2020/05/29/trump-writes-revoke-230-after-twitter-masks-tweets/

[152] *Center for Democracy & Technology v. Trump*, case # 20-1456 (D.C. Dist. Ct. 2020).

[153] Heater, Brian. "Republican senators ask FCC to examine Section 230, following Trump order" TechCrunch (2:13 pm PDT•June 9, 2020).

[154]
https://www.rubio.senate.gov/public/index.cfm/2020/6/rubio-loeffler-cramer-hawley-urge-fcc-to-clarify-section-230-protections-for-social-media-companies

[155] Hymes, Clare. "Justice Department recommends reforms to legal shield for tech companies." CBS News (June 17, 2020 / 5:17 PM)

[156] https://www.commerce.senate.gov/2017/5/video-pass-legislation-to-protect-the-open-internet

Cyber-Torts
Page 157

[157] Kosseff, Jeff. "Twenty Years of Intermediary Immunity: The U.S. Experience". 14:1. Scripted 5 (2017), https://script-ed.org/article/twenty-years-of-intermediary-immunity-the-us-experience/

[158] *Doe v. Backpage*, 817 F.3d 12, 15 (1st Cir. 2016) https://www.leagle.com/decision/infco20160314075; *but see Order on Motion to Dismiss, Doe v. Backpage*, Civil Action No. 17-11069-LTS (D. Mass., Mar. 29, 2018); https://www.leagle.com/decision/infdco20180330c00

[159] Citron, Danielle Keats. "Law's Expressive Value in Combating Cyber Gender Harassment". 108 Mich. L. Rev. 373 (2009).

[160] Rustad, Michael & Koenig, Thomas H. "The Tort of Negligent Enablement of Cybercrime, 20 Berkeley Tech. L.J. 1553, 1582 (2005). https://www.academia.edu/1601322/Tort_of_Negligent_E nablement_of_Cybercrime_The

[161] *see also* Rabin, Robert L. "Enabling Torts". 49 Depaul L. Rev. 435, 437 (1999) (arguing that there is little difference between inciting misconduct and enabling it).

[162] Citron, Danielle Keats. "Mainstreaming Privacy Torts". 98 Calif. L. Rev. 1805 (2010) (privacy invasions should be addressed by mainstream torts, including negligent enablement though section 230's broad immunity has often stood in the way).

[163] *Ibid.*

[164] Citron, Danielle Keats. Hate Crimes in Cyberspace (pp. 12-13). Harvard University Press. Kindle Edition.

Cyber-Torts

[165] Citron, Danielle Keats. Hate Crimes in Cyberspace (p. 19). (Harvard University Press, 2014).

[166] *Gertz v. Robert Welch, Inc.*, 418 U.S. 323, 94 S. Ct. 2997, 41 L. Ed. 2d 789 (1974); New York Times v. Sullivan, 376 U.S. 254, 84 S. Ct. 710, 11 L. Ed. 2d 686 (1964).

[167] *Braun v. Soldier of Fortune Magazine, Inc. et al.,* 968 F.2d 1110 (11th Cir. 1992).

[168] Margolick, David. "Slimed Online: Two Lawyers Fight Cyberbullying," Portfolio Magazine, February 11, 2009.

[169] Masnick, Mike. "More Details Emerge As States' Attorneys General Seek To Hold Back Innovation On The Internet. (from the this-is-a-bad-idea dept)" Techdirt.com (Jun 19th 2013 4:16pm) https://www.techdirt.com/articles/20130619/01031623524/more-details-emerge-as-states-attorneys-general-seek-to-hold-back-innovation-internet.shtml

[170] Solove, Daniel J. The Future of Reputation: Gossip, Rumor, and Privacy on the Internet (New Haven: Yale University Press, 2007), 130.

[171] *Varian Medical Systems, Inc. v. Delfino*, 6 Cal. Rptr. 3d 325, 337 (Ct. App. 2003).

[172] Ramsey, Aliah. "Internet Law – A Brief Introduction to Cyber Torts." (August 15, 2017). http://www.halsburylawchambers.com/internet-law-a-brief-introduction-to-cyber-torts/

[173] de León, Concepción. "Should the Internet Be

Cyber-Torts

Regulated?" N.Y. Times (Dec. 1, 2017).
https://www.nytimes.com/2017/12/01/books/net-neutrality-books.html

[174] Goldsmith, Jack and Wu, Tim. Who Controls the Internet? Illusions of a Borderless World. Oxford University Press. (2006)

[175] Riach, Duncan Ph.D. "Why the Internet Must Be Regulated." Hackernoon (December 15th 2017). https://hackernoon.com/why-the-internet-must-be-regulated-9d65031e7491

[176] Foer, Franklin. "It's Time to Regulate the Internet." The Atlantic (March 21, 2018). https://www.theatlantic.com/technology/archive/2018/03/its-time-to-regulate-the-internet/556097/

[177] Darlington, Roger. "How the Internet Could Be Regulated." http://www.rogerdarlington.me.uk/Internetregulation.html

[178] NPR Staff. "The Arab Spring: A Year of Revolution." NPR (December 17, 2011; 6:02 PM ET). https://www.npr.org/2011/12/17/143897126/the-arab-spring-a-year-of-revolution

[179] Alterman, Jon B. "A New Arab Spring?" CSIS (April 15, 2019). https://www.csis.org/analysis/new-arab-spring

[180] https://www.hg.org/internet-law.html

[181] Kosseff, Jeff. The Twenty-Six Words That Created the Internet . Cornell University Press. Kindle Edition.

[182] Black's Law Dictionary, 6th ed. (West, St. Paul, 1990).

Cyber-Torts

[183] Nix, Elizabeth. "When was the first U.S. driver's license issued?" History.com (Aug. 30, 2018).
https://www.history.com/news/when-was-the-first-u-s-drivers-license-issued

[184] *See Doe v. America Online*, 783 So.2d 1010, 1017 (Fl. 2001)

[185] *Batzel v. Smith*, 333 F.3d 1018, 1020 (9th Cir. 2003).

[186] *Batzel v. Smith*, 351 F. 3d 904, 907 (2003) (Gould, J., dissenting from denial of rehearing en banc).

[187] *Carafano v. Metrosplash*, 207 F. Supp. 2d 1055, 1066–67 (C.D. Cal. 2002).
Carafano v. Metrosplash, 339 F.3d 119, 1124 (9th Cir. 2003).

Books R. D. Kelly has published

R. D. Kelly has also published the following other books:

**A Poet Can Say Anything
by Bill Scribbler (2012)**

**Poems Volumes Two Through Five
by Bill Scribbler (2019)**

**Stories of Specific Lengths
By Bill Scribbler (2019)**

Available on Amazon.com:

https://www.amazon.com/s?i=digital-